After the People Vote

After the People Vote

A Guide to the Electoral College

Fourth Edition

Edited by John C. Fortier

THE AEI PRESS

Publisher for the American Enterprise Institute
Washington, DC

ISBN 978-0-8447-5033-0
      Hardback
      978-0-8447-5034-7
      Paperback
      978-0-8447-5035-4
      eBook

American Enterprise Institute
1789 Massachusetts Avenue, NW
Washington, DC 20036
www.aei.org

Contents

Introduction

This is the fourth edition of *After the People Vote*. The first edition was edited by Walter Berns, a teacher, mentor, and later AEI colleague of mine, who saw the need for a volume to explain how our system of electing a president works, especially the processes that kick in after the November general election date. Berns' constitutional scholarship and love of American institutions are omnipresent, not only in the two editions he edited but also in the two subsequent ones.

The mechanisms that lead to the final selection of a president are complex. Some procedures are sketched out in the original Constitution and its amendments, and others in federal law, congressional rules and procedures, state laws, and political party rules. These many processes are often loosely lumped under the heading "Electoral College." But the process of turning the people's votes on Election Day in November into a president in January involves not only selecting electors but also casting and counting electoral votes and resolving disputes and possible alternative scenarios resulting from vacancies in office or multiple candidates.

Interest in and controversy over the Electoral College go back to the early days of our republic. But the course of the four editions shows how the controversies of the day often shape particular concerns with the Electoral College. The first edition of *After the People Vote* followed an era when regionally strong third-party candidates had won electoral votes, raising the possibility that no candidate would receive a majority of electoral votes and presidential selection would be thrown to alternative congressional selection methods. The third edition followed the 2000 election, in which the Florida election dispute raised issues about how Congress might count electoral votes if they were disputed or if multiple slates of electors appeared. Today, the interest in the Electoral College is less about nontraditional selection procedures as much as concern that the Electoral

College vote and the national popular vote have diverged in two of our past five elections. And recent concerns about voting during the COVID-19 pandemic have raised questions about delays in the November 2020 election and how those delays might affect the processes that take place "after the people vote."

The core of *After the People Vote* has always been a series of questions about how the electoral process works. In the first edition, Berns thought through many of these questions and provided concise answers and analysis that shed light on possible election scenarios. In the second edition, Berns added two essays, one by Martin Diamond in defense of the Electoral College and one by AEI's Norman Ornstein on the history of three controversial elections: 1800, 1824, and 1876.

I edited the third edition and contributed an essay on the 2000 election controversy. I provided an excerpt from the original Martin Diamond essay, keeping the timeless parts but removing the material more specific to the 1960s and 1970s effort to amend the Constitution. To supplement that pro–Electoral College defense, Berns contributed a new essay. And law professors Akhil Reed Amar and Vikram David Amar penned a piece against the Electoral College.

This edition has two new contributions. As always, I have updated the central question section, but I have added several additional questions relating to how the Electoral College may be amended. In particular, there is today a movement to change the way we elect a president, not by the traditional constitutional amendment process but by persuading states to pass legislation that would select those states' electors based on the national popular vote rather than the popular vote in each state. This National Popular Vote effort and other ways of changing the Electoral College are detailed in the new section of questions.

The other significant addition is a chapter about public opinion on the Electoral College by AEI's Karlyn Bowman. Bowman is one of our nation's foremost scholars on the history of public opinion. She gives an encyclopedic account of Electoral College questions that pollsters have asked and how the public has responded.

For a four-decade-long project, there are many to thank. The contributors have all been referenced in this introduction. Special thanks are due to Karlyn Bowman and Norman Ornstein, not only for their contributions but also for their mentorship and encouragement over many years. My wife, Evelyn, has been a constant source of love, support, and insight for this edition and the previous one. Jason Grumet, president of the Bipartisan Policy Center, provided encouragement and support.

But this volume owes the most to Walter Berns, who did not live to see this fourth edition but whose spirit pervades its pages. Today, with two recent cases of a divergence of the popular and Electoral College vote, some wonder whether the elevated passions of our polarized politics would sow confusion and undermine the legitimacy of a close and contested election. For this reason, Berns' aim of writing *After the People Vote*—to elucidate the workings of institutions he admired—may be his greatest gift to a country he loved.

Timelines

TIMELINE FOR THE PRESIDENTIAL ELECTION OF 2020

November 3	Election Day
November 3–December 8	Period for resolving state recounts and controversies
December 14	Electors cast their votes
January 6	Congress counts the electors' votes
January 20	Inauguration Day

TIMELINE FOR THE PRESIDENTIAL ELECTION OF 2024

November 5	Election Day
November 5–December 10	Period for resolving state recounts and controversies
December 16	Electors cast their votes
January 6	Congress counts the electors' votes
January 20	Inauguration Day

TIMELINE FOR THE PRESIDENTIAL ELECTION OF 2028

November 7	Election Day
November 7–December 12	Period for resolving state recounts and controversies
December 18	Electors cast their votes
January 6	Congress counts the electors' votes
January 20	Inauguration Day

Part I

How the Electoral College Works

1

How Are the Electors Appointed?

November 3, 2020
November 5, 2024
November 7, 2028
First Tuesday after the first Monday of November

Although the millions of citizens who vote in the November election rightly think they are deciding who will be president, under Article II and the 23rd Amendment of the Constitution, only 538 persons are entitled to vote directly for the president and vice president. (See Appendix A.) Under prevailing state laws, these 538 electors are chosen by popular vote of the people of the states and the District of Columbia, and, except in Maine and Nebraska, they are chosen on a general-ticket (or winner-takes-all) basis.[1] The winning electors (or slate of electors) need capture only a plurality of the popular votes in each state.

How states choose their electors is, under Article II, Section 1, paragraph 2 of the Constitution, determined by state legislatures. (See Appendix A.) Congress may, by legislation, oversee the conduct of presidential elections, and the Constitution (whose rules may be enforced by the judiciary) has a good deal to say about voter eligibility in those elections. The Constitution does not, however, require electors to be chosen by popular vote of the people. In 1892, the Supreme Court recognized the states' authority to appoint electors.[2]

To repeat: By state law, electors in all states are chosen by popular vote, and (except in Maine and Nebraska) these popular votes are aggregated on a statewide basis. States may divide themselves into presidential-elector districts and aggregate the votes within each district or, like Maine and Nebraska, require some electors to be chosen in districts and some at large.

In either case, a state's electoral vote can be divided and cast for more than one presidential and vice-presidential candidate. In 2008,

Barack Obama lost the statewide vote in Nebraska but won the vote in the second district. John McCain received four of Nebraska's electors, and Obama received one. In 2016, Donald Trump lost the statewide vote in Maine but won the vote in the second district. Hillary Clinton received three of Maine's electors, and Trump received one. The states may also empower the governor to appoint electors, or they may authorize the legislature to appoint them.

Except in an extraordinary emergency, a state legislature is unlikely to stray from popular election of electors by assuming the power to appoint electors or by granting that power to the governor or any other person or group. Electors have been popularly elected since the Civil War. In fact, with only two exceptions, after 1828 the only state whose legislature chose the electors was South Carolina; its legislature did so through 1860. The exceptions were Florida in 1868, which had just been readmitted to the Union after the Civil War, and Colorado, which had been admitted to the Union close to Election Day in 1876. In both instances, the electors were chosen by the vote of the state legislatures.

Who Resolves Disputed Appointments?

As November 2000 demonstrated, election outcomes are not always known on election night. States must certify their results, and recounts and challenges are possible if the contest is close. States must conduct recounts and certify their vote totals in presidential elections in a much shorter time than in elections for other federal, state, or local offices.

Two key dates mark the end of the period for resolving election disputes. A federal statute provides that electors shall meet in their respective states to cast their votes on the first Monday after the second Wednesday in December of the election year, 41 days after the people cast their votes in November. The second, even more significant date further compresses the time states have to resolve disputes and was set by the Electoral Count Act of 1887.

This federal statute, still in effect today, was intended to prevent a recurrence of the events that followed the disputed Hayes-Tilden election of 1876. When Congress met to "count" the electoral votes after that election, it was confronted with two sets of electors—one voting for Hayes and the other for Tilden—from four states. The choice of a president turned on the issue of which votes were to be accepted and counted. Unable to agree, Congress appointed a 15-member electoral commission by an act approved by the president on January 29, 1877, almost three months after the election of electors. In due course and by a strictly partisan vote of eight to seven, the commission decided in favor of the Hayes electors, thus enabling Hayes to be elected president by a margin of one electoral vote.[3]

By enacting the Electoral Count Act of 1887, Congress decided that in the future states would resolve any such "controversy or contest" and that the states' determinations "shall be conclusive, and shall govern in the counting of the electoral votes as provided in the Constitution." (See Appendix B, Section 5.) The act accomplishes this by providing a "safe harbor" for each state to secure greater assurance that its slate of electors will not be challenged when Congress counts the votes. The statute provides that the persons designated electors by the states will be acknowledged by the Congress to be electors and eligible to vote in mid-December, for president and vice president, under the following conditions:

- If the state has a law governing the "determination of any controversy or contest" concerning the election of any or all of its presidential electors.

- If that law was enacted "prior to the day fixed for the appointment of the electors"—that is, on Election Day (November 3 in 2020, November 5 in 2024, and November 7 in 2028).

- If the determination of that controversy was made at least six days before the time fixed for the meeting of the electors (December 14 in 2020, December 16 in 2024, and December 18 in 2028).[4]

- If a state wants to take advantage of the greater protection afforded by this "safe harbor," the period to resolve disputes after Election Day shrinks to 35 days. This statute was of great significance in the 2000 election and was one of the reasons the Supreme Court became involved.

How the States Nominate and Bind Their Electors

As pointed out earlier, the presidential electors of each state are selected by procedures stipulated by its legislature. This section examines three aspects of these procedures: (1) how candidates for presidential electors are nominated, (2) whether the electors' names are printed on the ballots in November, and (3) whether the persons elected as presidential electors are bound by law to vote in the Electoral College for their parties' national nominees.

The procedures in each state are summarized in the table in Appendix C. The table shows considerable variation among the states in their manner of nominating candidates for presidential electors. Twenty-seven states stipulate that each party's candidates for electors be chosen by state party conventions, seven states and the District of Columbia require nomination by state or district party central committees, and 12 states let the parties use whatever methods they wish.

In addition, there is a smattering of other methods. In Arizona, the state party chairs select the slate of electors for the presidential party nominee. In California, the Democrats choose their elector candidates by having each Democratic nominee for the US House of Representatives designate one and each of the two most recent Democratic nominees for the US Senate designate one. For California Republicans, elector candidates are selected by the party's most recent nominees for the state constitutional offices and the US Senate, the party's leaders in each house of the state legislature, and various leaders of the state party organization.

In Pennsylvania, each party's national presidential nominee names the elector candidates on his or her party's ticket. In Wisconsin, each party's holdover members of both houses of the legislature, together with its candidates for the contested legislative seats, choose the elector candidates.

Forty-four states and the District of Columbia use the presidential short ballot, on which the names of the elector candidates do not appear.

The ballot shows each national party's presidential and vice-presidential candidates. The voter votes directly for one pair, and that vote is taken as a vote for all the elector candidates on that party's slate.

Three types of voting behavior are possible for electors. The "faithful elector" is pledged by state law or state party resolution to vote for his or her party's presidential and vice-presidential candidates and casts his or her electoral vote accordingly. The "faithless elector" is pledged in the same way but casts his or her electoral vote for others. The "unpledged elector," who is not pledged by law or party resolution to vote for any particular candidates, is legally free to vote for anyone he or she chooses.

Are the pledged presidential electors bound by law to vote in the Electoral College for the presidential and vice-presidential nominees who headed the slates on which the electors were elected? Eighteen states have no such requirement. Sixteen states and the District of Columbia say the electors are bound to vote for the national nominees heading their slate, but they provide no penalty for electors who do not. The remaining 16 states penalize electors who violate their pledges.

In 2004, as noted in the third edition of *After the People Vote*, only five states imposed penalties. All five imposed modest fines, and North Carolina added the provision that failure to vote as pledged shall constitute a resignation from the office of elector, that his or her vote not be recorded, and that another elector be appointed to cast the vote.

Recent years have seen many states add penalties for broken pledges. Some have added fines. Others have adopted a version of North Carolina's penalty, removing and replacing an elector for a "faithless" vote. In fact, the Uniform Law Commission developed model language for these "faithless elector" removal laws, and many states adopted the model or a similar version.

Today, two states provide for a fine only, 12 states provide for the replacement of "faithless electors," and two states both fine and replace a "faithless" elector. (In Colorado and Maine, the law does not provide for the removal and replacement of a "faithless elector," but the secretary of state claims the power to remove and replace.[5])

The matter is complicated by the actions states and courts took in the 2016 election and by a case recently decided by the Supreme Court. In 2016, electors in Colorado, Maine, and Minnesota attempted to cast "faithless" votes. In Colorado and Minnesota, the electors were removed and replaced; in Maine, an elector changed his vote to a faithful vote after his attempt to cast a faithless vote was ruled out of order. Later, a federal court ruled that the Colorado elector should not have been replaced. Four Washington state electors were fined for casting "faithless" votes. Lawsuits surrounding these practices made their way through the federal courts, and in May 2020, the Supreme Court heard two cases together: *Colorado Dept. of State v. Baca* on Colorado's removal and replacement of a "faithless elector" and *Chiafalo v. Washington* on Washington state's fining of "faithless electors." The Supreme Court upheld state laws that impose fines on "faithless electors" and state laws that replace an elector who attempts to vote unfaithfully with a new elector who can cast a faithful vote.

In the past, the number of electors who cast a vote for president that did not conform with the expected vote was quite small. Only 27 electors have cast such "faithless" votes for president throughout US history, although seven were cast in 2016.

The Supreme Court's decision preserves the current system in which some states have effectively prevented electors from casting faithless electors and other states have not. This system may complicate efforts to persuade electors to defect in order to change the outcome of the election or cast an elector for someone other than the major two party candidates, but these efforts could continue in the states without laws that replace electors for faithless votes.

2

For Whom Do Electors Vote?

December 14, 2020
December 16, 2024
December 18, 2028
First Monday after second Wednesday in December

Slates of electors are selected based on the popular vote for president in each state. Many electors, however, remain free—that is, not bound by the presidential vote. In many states, the electors are not bound at all; in other states that have attempted to bind their electors' votes, recent court decisions have called into question the validity of binding electors.

This freedom of the electors allows a good deal of room for bargaining between the November election and the meeting of the electors in mid-December if the election does not produce a majority in the Electoral College. For example, the electors for a third-party candidate who wins a plurality of the popular votes in one or more states could cast their ballots for one of the major-party candidates (or anyone else). In 1968, Hubert Humphrey could have asked his electors to vote for Richard Nixon, if Nixon had lacked an Electoral College majority, rather than see Nixon bargain with George Wallace. Thus, the Electoral College could well produce a winner in December who was not apparent on Election Day in November.

Also, an elector might vote for a person who would not have otherwise received votes in order for there to be a third candidate for Congress to consider if no person has a majority. In 2016, electors cast presidential votes for John Kasich and Colin Powell under the theory that they might be considered by the House of Representatives if neither Hillary Clinton nor Donald Trump received a majority of electors.

How the Ballots Are Cast

The electors appointed or chosen in November meet in their respective states in mid-December (December 14 in 2020, December 16 in 2024, and December 18 in 2028). Each elector casts two ballots, one for president and one for vice president. Although unknown to most of the public, the electors' names are certified by the governor of each state to an official of the federal government, the archivist of the United States. A federal statute requires that this be done "as soon as practicable" after the November election. (See Appendix B, Section 6.) Thus, shortly after the November election, assuming there is no prolonged controversy, an official of the national government knows the names of the 538 persons eligible to meet in their respective states and the District of Columbia in December to vote for president and vice president. He or she also knows the number of popular votes cast for the successful and unsuccessful candidates for electors.

The persons whose names appear in the certificates sent by the governors to Washington are the electors eligible to vote for president and vice president in December. As discussed in Chapter 1, any "controversy or contest" concerning the identity of these eligible electors should have been resolved by the states acting under state laws. The votes they cast, one for president and one for vice president, will be recorded in certificates, which will be sealed and sent to the president of the Senate and the archivist of the United States in Washington. (See Appendix B, Sections 9, 10, and 11.)

What If State Recounts Are Not Complete When the Electors Vote?

The statute that governs the electoral count gives states a large incentive to resolve their election controversies by six days before the electors vote, and, if they could not meet that "safe harbor" deadline, states would almost certainly try to resolve their election controversies by the day the electors vote, as they would risk losing their electoral votes otherwise.

There is, however, a precedent of a state missing these deadlines. In 1960, the vote between Nixon and John F. Kennedy was close in Hawaii. Initially, the election was certified for Nixon, electors were appointed, and they cast their votes for Nixon on the appointed day in mid-December. After a recount showed Kennedy to be the winner, the new results were certified on January 4, and a new slate of electors cast their votes for Kennedy. Vice President Nixon presided over the joint session of Congress that counted the votes and noted that while he had two slates of electors before him, the second one reflected political reality. He called for objections, and when there were none, he counted the Kennedy electors.[6]

While this precedent exists, it would be up to a future Congress to decide whether to accept a later slate of electors submitted by a governor over an earlier one. The 2000 election controversy showed how state recounts might extend beyond the "safe harbor" date or the day that the electors cast their votes. In 2000, the Florida legislature considered appointing a slate of electors because it feared that a state court would extend the recount beyond the "safe harbor" date. In reaction to the 2000 election, at least one state, North Carolina, amended its election laws to provide explicitly for the legislature to appoint a slate of electors directly if an election controversy were not resolved by six days before the electors cast their votes.

Must the President and the Vice President Be from Different States?

At least one of the two votes cast by electors must, of course, be cast for a person who is "not an inhabitant of the same state with themselves." This constitutional provision has led to the practice of political parties (and independent candidates) nominating a candidate for president from one state and a candidate for vice president from another. The Constitution does not require the president and vice president to be inhabitants of different states; it merely requires electors to cast at least one ballot for someone from a state other than their own.

Thus, if in 1980 the Republican Party had nominated Gerald Ford to run with his fellow Californian Ronald Reagan (assuming neither changed his official residence to another state), only California electors would have been presented with a problem and, more precisely, only California Republican electors. They would have had to vote for Reagan and, say, Jack Kemp or perhaps Kemp and Gerald Ford; they would not have been permitted to vote for a ticket comprising both Reagan and Ford. In a close election, this provision might mean that either the presidential or, more likely, the vice-presidential candidate might fail to achieve a majority of the Electoral College, and the election might be thrown to the House or Senate.

Practically, this issue is not likely to arise, for candidates can easily change their legal inhabitance. Immediately before becoming George W. Bush's running mate, Richard Cheney owned a house in Texas and was the CEO of a Houston-based company. Before the election, Cheney changed his legal residence to Wyoming, where he owned a house and had been raised and which he had represented in Congress. A group of Texas voters filed suit over the legitimacy of casting Texas electoral votes for Bush and Cheney.[7] The court ruled that an individual is an inhabitant of a given state if he "(1) has a physical presence within that state and (2) intends that it be his place of habitation."[8] As such, Wyoming fully qualified as Cheney's place of residence.

3

How Are the Electoral Votes Counted?

January 6

The certificates containing the votes cast in their respective states by the 538 electors in December are opened by the president of the Senate on January 6 before a joint session of the new House and the new Senate, the members of which (under the 20th Amendment of the Constitution) are themselves sworn in on January 3. (See Appendix A.) The certificates are identified and counted by tellers appointed by the House and the Senate and announced by state in alphabetical order.

According to the 12th Amendment of the Constitution (see Appendix A), the person having the greatest number of votes for president, if such a number is a majority of the electors appointed, shall be president, and the person having the greatest number of votes for vice president, if such a number is a majority of the electors appointed, shall be vice president. Assuming each state "appoints" the number of electors to which it is entitled, the total number of electors is 538, and the majority required for election is 270.

During the 2000 election controversy, the issue was raised as to what would happen if Florida did not appoint electors. The Florida Supreme Court ruled that several counties could have additional time beyond the legal deadline for completing initial recounts and ordered Secretary of State Katherine Harris not to certify the election results until a new court-ordered deadline. Had the court prevented the secretary of state from certifying election results at all, it is possible that no slate of electors would have been sent to Washington.

In that case, Congress, in counting the votes, would have found Al Gore with 267 (not counting a faithless elector) and George W. Bush with 246 electoral votes out of 513 electors appointed. Gore would have had a majority of the electors appointed and would have become president.

However, a slate of electors also could have been submitted by the Florida state legislature, which was contemplating such an action before the election controversy was resolved. And there would be controversies at the state level as to whether a court could prevent the governor from submitting a slate of electors.

Who Counts What?

On January 6, the tellers read "certificates and papers purporting to be certificates of the electoral votes." The president of the Senate calls for objections, if any, to these certificates or papers as they are read.[9] The electoral count statute (see Appendix B, Section 15) provides that objections must be made in writing; must state "clearly and concisely, and without argument, the ground thereof"; and must be signed by at least one member of the House and one member of the Senate.

When objections are filed, both houses retire to separate sessions to decide whether the questioned certificates are to be counted or rejected. Under the statute, both houses have to reject a challenged electoral ballot for the objection to prevail. The statute says that Congress shall not reject any "electoral vote or votes from any state which shall have been regularly given by electors whose appointment has been lawfully certified," but it does not define "regularly given." (See Appendix B, Section 15.)

These procedures were used for the first time on January 6, 1969. Rep. James O'Hara (D-MI), Sen. Edmund Muskie (D-ME), 37 other representatives, and six other senators objected in writing to the vote cast by Lloyd Bailey, a North Carolina elector who had been on the Republican slate but who voted for George Wallace and Curtis LeMay rather than Richard Nixon and Spiro Agnew. By roll-call votes, both houses rejected the challenge and upheld Bailey's vote.

On January 6, 2001, Democratic House members lodged 20 objections, but none received a senator's support, which was required for the objection to be considered by the two houses of Congress. Most recently, on January 6, 2017, House Democrats raised 11 objections, but none received a senator's support.

It might be concluded from the 1969 example that a "regularly given vote"—which is a vote the Congress must count—means nothing more than a vote cast by an elector whose name had been certified by the governor of the state to the archivist of the United States. Under this interpretation, a list of certified electors from each state will on January 6 be in the hands of the Congress, whose only function is to see that the votes were cast by the electors whose names appear on those lists.

The term "regularly given" could, however, be interpreted more expansively by a future Congress, especially a Congress confronted with faithless electors whose votes, unlike Bailey's, would determine an election's outcome. The term does, after all, appear in the 1887 statute written by Congress. But if Congress were to refuse to count a vote cast by a faithless elector—for example, a vote cast for a third-party candidate by an elector pledged to vote for a Republican or Democratic candidate—it would be interpreting more than statutory language; it would be making a constitutional judgment.

Before the 1887 law, some authorities (including Abraham Lincoln) understood that the power to resolve disputes concerning what electoral votes to count belonged exclusively to Congress. In his Message to Congress of February 8, 1865, President Lincoln wrote:

> The joint resolution, entitled "Joint Resolution declaring certain States not entitled to representation in the electoral college," has been signed by the executive, in deference to the view implied in its passage and presentation to him. In his own view, however, the two Houses of Congress, convened under the twelfth article of the Constitution, have complete power to exclude from counting all electoral votes deemed by them to be illegal; and it is not competent for the executive to defeat or obstruct that power by a veto, as would be the case if his action were at all essential to the matter. He disclaims all right of the executive to interfere in any way in the matter of canvassing or counting electoral votes.[10]

If the November election's results are disputed and Congress receives more than one list of electors, and if that dispute has not been resolved according to the state's laws, then the two houses, acting concurrently, decide who are the eligible electors. (See Appendix B, Section 5.) In the case of a disagreement between the two houses over which slate of electors is valid, federal law provides that Congress should count the one certified by the governor. It does not, however, give Congress guidance on how to choose between two slates of electors submitted by the governor.

If, in 2000, the recount had continued and put Gore in the lead, a state court might have compelled the governor of Florida to appoint a slate of electors for Gore in addition to the Bush slate that the governor had appointed after the initial certification of the election. It would have been up to Congress to choose which slate to accept.

4

What If No One Has a Majority?

January 20

Once the Congress has met and counted and certified the electoral votes, the 12th Amendment of the Constitution sets the basic provisions for making a decision if no presidential candidate has received the requisite majority.

> From the persons having the highest numbers not exceeding three on the list of those voted for as President, the House of Representatives shall choose immediately, by ballot, the President. But in choosing the President, the votes shall be taken by states, the representation from each state having one vote; a quorum for this purpose shall consist of a member or members from two-thirds of the states, and a majority of all the states shall be necessary to a choice.

The House Chooses a President

Should a presidential election be thrown to Congress for decision, there are precedents, rules, laws, and procedures for making the decision—but also much room for the particular Congress to determine its own format and rules.

Provisions in the 12th and 20th Amendments of the Constitution determine the basic role of the House of Representatives in this process. Regarding the mechanics of the House decision, the House, as in other matters, sets its own rules and procedures. The precedents set by the House in February 1825 in deciding the election of 1824 provide some guidance.

(See Appendix D.) The House could follow these precedents or, if it wished, ignore them and draw up new procedures.

The new procedures would be unlikely to differ greatly from the 1825 set, except in one key respect: In 1825, the old, or lame-duck, House made the presidential selection. The difference between 1825 and today is that the adoption of the 20th Amendment in 1933 changed the dates that members of Congress and the president begin their terms of office. Today, Congress comes into session before the president takes office and before the January 6 date set by statute for counting the electoral votes in Congress. Before 1933, the old Congress would remain in session to count the electoral votes, the president-elect would not take office until March 4, and the new Congress would not come into session until December unless called into session by the president or unless Congress, by law, set an earlier date.

As the January 6 date is set by statute, Congress could conceivably change the law and set the date back, empowering the old Congress to make the presidential decision. That is most unlikely, however, particularly since the record of deliberation on the 20th Amendment reflects a clear intention to have this decision in the hands of the new Congress.

Of the specific precedents from 1825, one is of particular significance: the requirement of a majority of a state's whole delegation to vote for a candidate in order for the state vote to be cast. If no candidate got a majority, the state was recorded as divided, and no vote was cast.

In the 107th Congress, which counted the electoral votes after the 2000 presidential election, 28 state delegations had Republican majorities, 17 had Democratic majorities, four were divided evenly, and, again, Vermont had one independent. Had three Republican representatives lost their elections, say in Colorado, Indiana, and Pennsylvania, no party would have controlled the 26 delegations necessary to elect a president in the House of Representatives. As it was, during the election controversy, Republicans knew that if no candidate secured a majority of the electors, they would likely have had the votes to elect a president. While representatives are free to vote their conscience, not their party, party preference likely would have prevailed in the House.

The Senate Chooses a Vice President

The 12th Amendment of the Constitution also sets the basic provisions for decision if no vice-presidential candidate has received the requisite majority of electoral votes.

> From the two highest numbers on the list, the Senate shall choose the Vice President; a quorum for the purpose shall consist of two-thirds of the whole number of Senators, and a majority of the whole number shall be necessary to a choice.

The Senate has selected a vice president once, in 1837. Because of a personal scandal, President-elect Martin Van Buren's running mate, Richard Johnson, received one fewer than a majority of electoral votes but was elected by the Senate.

Unlike members of the House, senators vote as individuals, not as part of a state delegation, and, as noted above, they choose between the top two candidates, not among the top three. Moreover, the requirements for a quorum in the Senate—two-thirds of the full Senate, or, at present, 67 senators—are more stringent than in the House, where only one member from two-thirds of the states is needed. Thus, a boycott by members of one party in the Senate could prevent a choice of vice president, if that party had more than the 34 senators needed to block a quorum.

5

What If No One Has Been Chosen by Inauguration Day?

The 20th Amendment of the Constitution fixes the end of the terms of the president and vice president at noon on January 20. If a president has been chosen by that time, he or she will be sworn in. If a president has not been chosen, but there is a vice president elect, the vice president elect becomes acting president until the House selects the president in the manner described earlier.

*

The Presidential Succession Act

The Presidential Succession Act of 1947 (see Appendix B, Section 19) comes into play under any of the following conditions:

- If the House fails to choose a president and the Senate fails to choose a vice president;

- If the president-elect and vice president elect both die, they both become incapacitated, or one dies and the other becomes incapacitated; or

- If both are discovered after January 6 to be constitutionally unqualified to hold office.[11]

The next in line after the vice president to serve as acting president is the Speaker of the House, who in turn is followed by the president pro tempore of the Senate. They may act as president, however, only if they meet the legal requirements for the presidency, spelled out in Article II of the Constitution. In addition, Article I of the Constitution bars members of the House and Senate from holding any other federal office. The Presidential Succession Act specifically interprets this to mean that the Speaker or president pro tempore must resign from his or her leadership office and seat in the House or Senate to serve as acting president.

Because the Presidential Succession Act requires the acting president to relinquish that position as soon as a president or vice president is chosen, the Speaker and president pro tempore might well choose not to resign from Congress to become acting president. If that happens, the process then moves on to qualified cabinet officers in the following order: secretaries of state, treasury, and defense; attorney general; and secretaries of interior, agriculture, commerce, labor, health and human services, housing and urban development, transportation, energy, education, veterans' affairs, and homeland security.

Since cabinet officers stay in office until they resign or are discharged by the president, the person who would become acting president under this set of contingencies would be a cabinet officer from the previous administration. If the 2000 election controversy had continued until Inauguration Day with no president-elect or vice president elect chosen, the United States might have found itself with Acting President Lawrence Summers, the treasury secretary in the Bill Clinton administration, through the following chain of circumstances.

Speaker of the House Dennis Hastert could have acted as president, but only by resigning his Speakership and seat in Congress, which he may well have been unwilling to do as he would not be able to resume them upon the eventual selection of a president by the Congress. Next in line was the president pro tempore of the Senate, who might also have declined the presidency rather than resign from the Senate. In January 2001, that office was held by Sen. Robert Byrd (D-WV).

The Senate was split 50–50, with the tie being broken by Vice President Gore (until January 20, when Vice President Cheney would then break the tie for the Republicans). Had the Republicans controlled the Senate in January, the 99-year-old Strom Thurmond would have been next in the line of succession and surely would not have been able to serve as acting president. The secretary of state remaining in office from the Clinton administration, Madeleine Albright, would have been next in line, but she could not serve as president as she was not a natural-born citizen. The presidency, then, might have fallen to Secretary Summers.

Only an officer confirmed by the Senate (not, for example, a secretary appointed as a recess appointment) and not under impeachment by the House may become acting president. Confirmed cabinet officers are passed over if they fail to qualify as president, and subsequent qualification of an officer thus passed over (such as by turning 35 or reaching his or her 14th year of residency in this country) does not result in a change of acting president.

A later decision by a qualified Speaker or president pro tempore to resign from Congress would, however, displace the former cabinet officer and make the Speaker or president pro tempore the acting president until a vice president or president is named or until the presidential term expires, whichever comes first. To take our earlier example, if Secretary of the Treasury Summers had become acting president, and, subsequently, Speaker of the House Hastert had changed his mind about declining the presidency, Speaker Hastert would have bumped Secretary Summers and become acting president until a president or vice president was selected or the presidential term ended.

6

What If a Major-Party Candidate Dies or Resigns?

If a candidate nominated by a political party dies or resigns before the date fixed for the choice of presidential electors (that is, Election Day in November), the national committee of the affected party meets and chooses a new presidential or vice-presidential candidate. Article III of the Charter and Bylaws of the Democratic Party and rule 9 of the Rules of the Republican Party permit the national committees so to act. (See Appendix E.)

In 1912, both President William H. Taft and Vice President James S. Sherman were renominated at the June Republican convention. Vice President Sherman died October 30, and the Republican National Committee chose another candidate, but not until after the November election. The committee substituted Nicholas Murray Butler, and the eight Republican electors cast their ballots for him in the December voting.

On July 13, 1972, Sen. Thomas Eagleton was nominated as the candidate for vice president at the Democratic National Convention. Stories began circulating almost immediately about Sen. Eagleton's problems of mental strain some years before and his three hospitalizations. At first, presidential nominee George McGovern supported Eagleton's continuation on the ticket, but Sen. Eagleton finally withdrew at the end of July. On August 8, the Democratic National Committee substituted R. Sargent Shriver as the new nominee for vice president.

Death or Resignation After the Election

If the death or resignation occurs between the November election and mid-December, the day the electors cast their ballots, the national committee of the party affected will probably proceed as it would if the candidate died or resigned before the November election—assuming there is time to convene the committee. In any event, no legal problem would arise because (leaving aside the question of electors bound by state law to cast a ballot for a named candidate) the electors, under the Constitution, are free to vote for whomever they choose.

Note, however, that in recent years some states have enacted stronger laws to bind electors by replacing faithless electors with faithful ones. The Supreme Court affirmed states' ability to enact such laws, but it also noted that in the candidate's death, a strict binding of electors' votes would complicate a party's ability to instruct electors to vote for a replacement to a deceased candidate. The Court also noted that several of these laws had exceptions in which they removed the binding of the elector in the case of a candidate's death. But many of the laws do not have this exception, so a political party might not be able to coalesce around a replacement for a deceased candidate as it had been able to in the past.[12]

If the death or resignation occurs between January 6 and January 20, the case will be governed by the 20th Amendment of the Constitution. Section 3 of the amendment reads:

> If, at the time fixed for the beginning of the term of the President, the President elect shall have died, the Vice President elect shall become President . . . and the Congress may by law provide for the case wherein neither a President elect nor a Vice President elect shall have qualified, declaring who shall then act as President, or the manner in which one who is to act shall be selected.

Thus, if both the president-elect and the vice president elect were to die during this period, the law enacted by Congress under the authority of this amendment (the Presidential Succession Act) would take effect. (See Appendix B, Section 19.)

There is some question concerning the consequences if the death occurs between mid-December and January 6. Will there be a president-elect and a vice president elect during this period? If so, the 20th Amendment governs the case. If the president-elect dies, the person receiving the majority of electoral votes cast for vice president—or, if no one receives a majority, the person chosen by the Senate on January 6 to be vice president—becomes president. In either case, that person will be vice president elect, and, as the 20th Amendment says, if, at the time fixed for the beginning of the term of the president, the president-elect shall have died, "the Vice President elect shall become President."

Formally, there will be no president-elect, however, until the electoral votes are counted and announced by Congress on January 6. Although the electors will have voted and the country will know—or will think it knows—whether anyone has received a majority, those votes will be under seal and will not be known officially until Congress opens them.

Whether there is a president-elect or not will depend on Congress when it counts the votes. Congress has two courses of action if faced with a presidential candidate who has received a majority of votes from the presidential electors but has died or resigned before those votes have been counted by Congress. First, Congress could choose to count the votes for the deceased or resigned presidential candidate, thereby making him or her the president-elect (even if deceased). Then the provision of the 20th Amendment, by which a vice president elect is sworn in as president on January 20 if the president-elect has died, will take effect.

Congress, however, might not recognize votes for the deceased candidate, as it did in 1872 with votes for Horace Greeley, who died after Election Day but before the electors cast their votes.[13] If there are sufficient votes to reject these electors, the Congress is then faced with a situation in which no candidate has a majority of the Electoral College. In this case, it is left to the House of Representatives to pick from among the three candidates who has received the highest number of electoral votes.

What Is Not Covered

According to Section 4 of the 20th Amendment:

Congress may by law provide for the case of the death of any of the persons from whom the House of Representatives may choose a President whenever the right of choice shall have devolved upon them, and for the case of the death of any of the persons from whom the Senate may choose a Vice President whenever the right of choice shall have devolved upon them.

Unfortunately, Congress has not enacted such a law. The Presidential Succession Act, authorized by Section 3 of the 20th Amendment, meets the cases of the death of a president or president-elect, but not the cases of the death "of any of the persons" from whom the House and Senate may choose a president or vice president. In enacting the Presidential Succession Act, Congress may have thought it was providing for the case of the death of any of the persons from whom the House may choose a president and the Senate a vice president. If the reading here given to the terms "president-elect" and "vice president elect" is correct, however, the act does not cover that case.

Congress could, of course, choose to ignore the winning candidate's death and proceed to name him or her president-elect. Then, the president-elect having died, the vice president elect would, under the 20th Amendment, become president. Congress might reason that this outcome is in accordance with the popular will or, at least, does not thwart it.

7

Changing the Electoral College

From nearly the beginning of our republic, there have been efforts to abolish or reform the Electoral College. The traditional avenue for change has been a constitutional amendment. The 12th Amendment was ratified in the aftermath of the election of 1800 and changed the way our electoral system operated. Similarly, efforts to move to a direct national popular vote have often been proposed as constitutional amendments.

In recent years, proponents of changing our Electoral College system have pursued a new avenue for change, the National Popular Vote Initiative, which advocates for an indirect method of moving to a popular vote by persuading state legislatures to change the way they allocate their electors.

Finally, while much of what is thought of as the "Electoral College" is in the Constitution, some parts of our system are in law, custom, or party or legislative rules and could be changed without a constitutional amendment. For example, the dates of the electors' meeting and the congressional counting of the electors' votes are set by statute, not by the Constitution. The November general election date, the December "safe harbor" date, and the December meeting date of the electors are set by statute. The current compressed time frame of these dates means that any delay of Election Day due to an emergency or delays in counting the vote risks the possibility that the electors might not be able to cast their votes. These dates, however, could be changed by statute to allow more time to resolve an election.

Changing the Electoral College by Constitutional Amendment

As much of the Electoral College machinery is laid out in the Constitution, constitutional amendment has been a common method for reform. In the 1800 election, aspects of the original system caused what we would consider today the winning presidential and vice-presidential candidates ending up in an electoral tie. In the aftermath of that election, Congress passed and sufficient states ratified the 12th Amendment, which required electors to specify a vote for president and another for vice president and clarified the system for resolving ties or other situations when no candidate has a majority of electors.

Various constitutional amendments have been introduced in Congress to move to a system based on the national popular vote. In 1969, during the 91st Congress, the House of Representatives voted in favor of such an amendment by more than the two-thirds required. The Senate, however, did not pass the amendment, and it was not sent to the states for ratification.

Changing the Electoral College by a constitutional amendment is difficult, as it requires a supermajority in Congress and the states.

The National Popular Vote Initiative

After the 2000 election, some opponents of the Electoral College began to consider a new avenue for reform. The National Popular Vote Initiative began to advocate for a way to move to a national popular vote without a constitutional amendment.

The effort relies on the insight that states have great freedom in deciding how they select electors who will cast a vote for president and vice president. Currently, all but two states hold a popular election in their states that will elect a slate of electors loyal to the political candidate and party that wins the statewide popular election. In the past, however, state legislatures have appointed the electors directly, and there have been a variety of district systems that allocate electors based on the popular vote in part of a state.

The National Popular Vote Initiative advocates for a system in which states allocate their electors according to the results of the national popular vote rather than the results of their own state's popular vote. For example, if a plurality of Pennsylvania voters voted for candidate X, but a plurality of nationwide voters supported candidate Y, then Pennsylvania would select a slate of electors loyal to candidate Y, even though its own voters had supported candidate X.

These reformers have advocated for these laws in a number of states. If enough states pass such laws (enough states where the total of these states' electors adds up to a minimum of 270 electors), then the winner of the national popular vote will automatically get assigned a majority of electors. The state legislation also calls on a state to enter a compact with other states that have passed this legislation to ensure greater permanence and stability.

Advocates of these proposals argue that they are constitutional, as they rely on the state's ability to choose the method by which it allocates electors.[14] Critics of the proposal question whether a state may allocate its electors to a measure that is not related to their own state's choice of president. They also question the compact and certain logistical issues such as how recounts would be held.[15]

As of the publication of this volume, 15 states and the District of Columbia, adding up to 196 electoral votes, have passed legislation. Additional states totaling 74 electors or more would be needed for the compact to reach the threshold of a majority of the electors to be decided by the national popular vote.[16] Colorado, which has already enacted the National Popular Vote plan, will vote in November 2020 whether to keep or repeal the initiative.

Part II

The History of Disputed Elections

8

Three Disputed Elections:
1800, 1824, and 1876

Norman J. Ornstein

Before 2000, three presidential elections in American history had raised both controversy and constitutional question marks—the elections of 1800, 1824, and 1876.[17] The controversy in 1800 resulted in a constitutional amendment, and the one in 1876 resulted in two major pieces of legislation to change the processes for counting electoral votes and for presidential succession.

The Election of 1800

The original Constitution did not provide for separate ballots for president and vice president. Electors voted for two candidates, and the candidate who received the most electoral votes (if a majority) became president, while the one finishing second became vice president. If two candidates tied with the votes of a majority of electors, then the House of Representatives would vote to break the tie.[18]

In 1800, the Federalist Party's congressional caucus nominated John Adams as its presidential candidate for a second term and South Carolina's Charles Cotesworth Pinckney as his running mate. Pinckney's brother, Thomas Pinckney, had been paired with Adams in 1796 but had fallen short of second place in the electoral vote. The Democratic-Republican Thomas Jefferson had therefore been elected vice president.

The congressional caucus of the Democratic-Republican Party nominated Vice President Thomas Jefferson for president in the 1800 election, pairing him with Aaron Burr. After the electors assembled in their respective states on December 4, it became clear that the Democratic-Republicans had prevailed, but Jefferson and Burr received an equal number of electoral votes, 73. Adams received 65 and Pinckney, 64.

The presidency, therefore, had to be decided by a lame-duck House of Representatives, which still had a Federalist majority. Rather than following the Democratic-Republican Party's choice for president, the Federalists complicated the selection with mischief making and political maneuvering.

Because Thomas Jefferson was the most visible and capable foe of the Federalists, there was substantial sentiment in the party to pass him by and give the presidency to Burr, a man they saw as less formidable and more pliable. At the same time, the party would be sowing deep dissension within the opposition. But the patriotism and honor of Federalist Alexander Hamilton ultimately prevented that strategy from succeeding. Hamilton's personal relationship with Burr at that time was quite cordial, while his relationship with Jefferson was bitter. Hamilton wrote, "If there be a man in the world I ought to hate, it is Jefferson. With Burr I have always been personally well. But the public good must be paramount to every private consideration."[19]

Congress assembled on February 11, 1801, for the electoral count. As the vice president and presiding officer of the Senate, Jefferson received the votes from the tellers and announced them. Georgia's electoral votes were not authenticated by the electors' signatures, either outside or inside the envelope, which merely contained a statement that four votes had been cast for Jefferson and Burr. Uncertain how to handle this, the tellers handed the envelope to Jefferson, who declared that Georgia had cast four votes for him and four votes for Burr, avoiding any interpretation that might have favored him or cast additional doubt on the vote.

The formal count in the House thus replicated the earlier reports, and the House itself began to vote. The 106-member House of Representatives had 58 Federalists and 48 Democratic-Republicans at the time; had the vote been by member, there is little doubt that Burr would have won. But the Constitution provided that the votes would be cast by states.

On the first ballot, Jefferson won eight states and Burr, six. Two states, Maryland and Vermont, were equally divided. From February 11 to February 17, 35 votes were taken with the same result. The opportunities for vote trading and influence peddling were enormous, but neither candidate succumbed or succeeded.

Hamilton's influence finally broke the logjam. On the 36th ballot, many Federalists declined to vote. The two deadlocked states went for Jefferson, while Delaware and South Carolina, previously for Burr, now deadlocked themselves. The final count was 10 states for Jefferson and four states, all in New England, for Burr. Burr automatically became vice president.

A few years later, after Hamilton had intervened in New York politics to stop Burr once again, their personal relationship deteriorated until they met in a duel—perhaps the most infamous in American history—which resulted in the tragic death of Founding Father Alexander Hamilton.

The dangers inherent in the original system of double balloting became clear with the Jefferson-Burr controversy. Momentum for passing an amendment to allow separate electoral votes for president and vice president began to build immediately after the vote in the House. The 12th Amendment to the Constitution was approved by Congress in December 1803 and ratified by the states in time for the next presidential election.

The Election of 1824

Five serious contenders emerged for the presidency as 1824 approached: John C. Calhoun and William H. Crawford from the South, John Quincy Adams from the Northeast, and Henry Clay and Andrew Jackson from the West. Calhoun dropped out of consideration in 1824 to run for vice president, leaving four. William H. Crawford of Georgia was treasury secretary under President James Monroe. He received the Republican congressional caucus nomination, but with only 66 of the Republican members of Congress in attendance, barely a third of the total, the nomination was widely attacked as illegitimate and unconstitutional; at the same time, a number of newspapers attacked the power of "King Caucus" in general. The other presidential candidates received their nominations through other avenues: Adams was nominated by the legislatures of several states in New England, Clay was picked by the Kentucky legislature, and Jackson was nominated by the Tennessee legislature and by nominating conventions held across the country.

In a campaign characterized more by questions of personality than issues and dominated by personal attacks on the candidates by partisan newspapers, no single strong candidate for president emerged. Twenty-four states cast electoral votes; 131 votes were necessary for a majority. Andrew Jackson led with 99, polling 152,901 popular votes (44.3 percent of those cast); he carried Pennsylvania, New Jersey, most of the South, and the new West, except for Ohio. Adams received 84 electoral votes and 114,023 popular votes (30 percent), carrying New York and New England. Crawford received 41 electoral votes, carrying Georgia, Virginia, and eight scattered others.

Clay, to his bitter disappointment, finished fourth, four electoral votes behind Crawford despite winning more popular votes than the treasury secretary (13.2 percent to 12.5 percent). Clay won all the electoral votes of Ohio, Missouri, and his home state, Kentucky, and four from New York. Had Clay, the veteran Speaker of the House, received only three electoral votes from the hodgepodge of electors who went for the ill and paralytic Crawford—and questions were raised about the legitimacy of several of those votes—he would without doubt have been elected president by the House of Representatives. But the Constitution limited the choice to the top three candidates, rendering him ineligible.

In January 1825, the contest shifted to the House, which proceeded to ballot by state. No rules existed for the vote, so the House directed each state vote to be cast according to the preference of an absolute majority of the state's congressmen.

Although the Speaker, Henry Clay, had been deprived through political machinations of a chance at the prize, his role was far from over. Clay was not a strong admirer of any of the three choices, but he eagerly assumed the role of kingmaker. Crawford's health condition removed him from serious consideration, even though his issue positions were closest to Clay's. Clay had opposed Adams regularly during Adams' tenure as Monroe's secretary of state, although they agreed on the Monroe Doctrine. Jackson assiduously courted Clay, but, to Clay, he was not a trained statesman, sophisticated in the ways of statecraft, while Adams, despite their differences, was.

Clay met with Adams on Sunday evening, January 9, and soon rumors were circulating that Clay had been promised the State Department if he delivered the votes of Ohio and Kentucky—states Clay had won in the election. Clay denied the charges, calling his accuser "a base and infamous calumniator, a dastard, and a liar."[20] Nevertheless, on January 24, Clay and a majority of the Ohio and Kentucky delegates announced their support for Adams.

Several states, though committed to Adams on the first ballot, meant to defect to Jackson on a later round of voting. To win, Adams needed a first ballot victory, and New York's vote would ensure it. But the New York delegation was split. The deciding ballot was in the hands of kindly old Stephen Van Rensselaer, who had pledged support to all three candidates. In the end, with some help from Daniel Webster, Adams managed to win Van Rensselaer's vote—and with it the White House.

Later Van Rensselaer claimed that divine intervention, not pressure, prompted his vote for Adams. As New York began to vote, he claimed, he had bent his head in prayer and spied on the floor a ballot for Adams. He took this as a sign from heaven and voted accordingly.

Soon thereafter, Henry Clay was named secretary of state. Although much evidence would suggest that Clay's support for Adams had other, legitimate roots, this did not stop an uproar of protest. Sen. John Randolph of Virginia was so outraged that he hurled public insults at Clay, calling him a "blackleg," the term for a dishonest gambler. In response to this public humiliation, Clay and Randolph met in a duel on the banks of the Potomac, armed with pistols, each accompanied by seconds and a surgeon. Shots were fired, but the only casualty was the skirt of Randolph's coat. The duelers then chose to settle their differences with a handshake, and within a week they had exchanged cards and resumed social relations.

Jackson did not resume any relationship with Clay. He bitterly wrote friends, "Was there ever such a bare-faced corruption in any country before?"[21] Four years later, Jackson, running a populist campaign against the sort of backroom politics that had elected Adams, won the presidential election of 1828 by a landslide.

The Election of 1876

The election of 1876, ironically America's centennial year, was perhaps the most controversial in American history. It was not decided in the House of Representatives, but rather by a special electoral commission formed to settle a controversy over disputed electoral votes.

At their conventions, the Republicans and the Democrats both picked as their candidates well-respected reform governors. The Republicans, meeting in Cincinnati, chose Ohio Gov. Rutherford B. Hayes, known for his opposition to the spoils system. The Democrats, meeting in St. Louis, picked New York Gov. Samuel J. Tilden, who had broken both Tammany Hall and the infamous Canal Ring.

The two candidates' positions on the top issues of the time had few major differences. The campaign, focusing on personalities, became bitter and dirty. Each side hurled insults and lies at the other. Hayes was accused of stealing the pay of dead soldiers during the Civil War and shooting his mother in a fit of insanity, while Tilden, among other things, was called a drunkard, a thief, syphilitic, a liar, and a swindler.

In the aftermath of the election, it appeared Tilden had won. He received 264,000 more popular votes than Hayes and outdistanced him in electoral votes by 184 to 165. With 20 electoral votes still outstanding and 185 required to win, Tilden needed only one more to clinch a victory. Even Hayes thought he had lost the election when he retired on election night.

But the leadership of the Republican Party was unwilling to give up. Party chairman Zachariah Chandler and his associates began to exert pressure on the remaining states—South Carolina, Florida, and Louisiana—and on one of Oregon's three votes. Hayes supporter Gen. Daniel Sickles sent out a telegram over Chandler's name to officials in these four states that read, "With your state sure for Hayes, he is elected. Hold your state."[22]

Chandler then claimed that Hayes had 185 electoral votes and was elected president. Near chaos ensued. President Ulysses S. Grant had to send troops to keep the peace in areas where the votes were being tabulated. There was bribery, forgery, and ballot-box stuffing on both sides. In the end, multiple sets of returns were sent to Washington from the three southern states involved. The struggle over the disputed votes lasted from Election Day, November 8, 1876, until March 2, 1877.

The Constitution does not outline specific procedures to be followed in the case of conflicting returns from any state. The Democratic House of Representatives would not agree to let the Senate president, a Republican, arbitrate, nor would the Republican Senate leave the decision to the Democratic House.

Congress compromised by creating a 15-member bipartisan electoral commission, consisting of five senators, five representatives, and five Supreme Court justices, to decide which candidate had won the disputed votes. Seven members of the commission were to be Democrats and seven Republicans, while the 15th vote would be cast by Justice David Davis, universally regarded as an independent. At the last minute, however, Davis was elected to the Senate by the Illinois legislature and became ineligible. The Republican justice Joseph Bradley replaced him. Although the Democrats believed he would be nonpartisan, Bradley voted with his Republican colleagues on every significant question. Thus, the commission split eight to seven consistently in favor of Hayes.

The electoral count began in Congress on February 1 (changed from the second Wednesday in February for this one election), and the proceedings continued until March 2. States were called in alphabetical order. When a disputed state was called, objections were raised to both Tilden and Hayes electors. The question was then referred to the electoral commission; in every instance, it voted eight to seven for Hayes. The Democratic House rejected the commission's decision, but the Republican Senate upheld it. And, under the rules, the decision stood.

The country ultimately acquiesced in the decision, as did Tilden, who nonetheless believed until his death that he had been duly elected president. Serious violence, however, nearly marred this election. Justice Bradley's life was threatened, and his house had to be placed under guard. Hayes, too, was threatened and even fired on one night while eating dinner with his family. The bullet missed Hayes and lodged in the library wall. Northern Democrats were enraged by the electoral commission's actions, and the House of Representatives launched an investigation, which found flagrant fraud by Republicans in the South—but also uncovered instances of Democratic bribery and vote abuse.

The real end to the crisis came with the Compromise of 1877, in which southern Democrats accepted the electoral commission's result and Hayes promised to end Reconstruction by removing Republican carpetbag governments from southern states. Southern Democratic promises to protect the interests of African Americans in their states were soon ignored, and the post–Civil War era, along with civil rights, came to an end.

A decade later, in 1887, Congress finally settled on a procedure for disputed electoral votes. (See Appendix B.) The Electoral Count Act placed the final authority in the states themselves for determining the validity and legality of their choice of electors. A concurrent majority in both houses of Congress would be required to reject any electoral votes.

9

The 2000 Election

John C. Fortier

The polls on the eve of Election Day, November 7, 2000, showed a close race between George W. Bush and Al Gore.[23] Bush had held a small but consistent lead of 4–5 percent in the polls since October, but in the final days before the election, the race closed to a dead heat. Some wrongly surmised that Bush might win the popular vote while losing a majority of the Electoral College, but no pundits could have predicted what would unfold that night and in the 36 days afterward.

Just before 8:00 p.m. Eastern Standard Time, the television networks and the Associated Press called the result in Florida as a victory for Al Gore. This large and key state (with 25 electoral votes at the time) was a big enough prize that many television commentators suggested Gore's win there would make him the 43rd president of the United States. But despite these early prognostications, not all the polls had closed in Florida, nor in many other states.

Just after 10:00 p.m., the Voter News Service (a consortium of news organizations that conducted the exit polls) retracted its call of Florida for Gore, declaring the contest "too close to call." In the wee hours of the following morning, projections began to show that George W. Bush would win Florida. At 2:13 a.m., Fox News, followed by the other networks, called Florida for Bush. By this time, it was apparent that a Bush victory in Florida would be sufficient to guarantee him a majority in the Electoral College.

Vice President Gore also believed this to be the case when he phoned Bush to concede the election at 2:30 a.m., and he readied himself to deliver a concession speech to his supporters gathered at the Nashville War Memorial. On the drive to the speech, several of Gore's advisers continued to follow the official Florida vote counts and noticed Bush's seemingly insuperable margin of victory evaporating. They urgently phoned the vice president to alert him to this development minutes before he was to deliver his concession speech. At 3:30 a.m., Gore phoned Bush and retracted the concession he had made just an hour earlier. The election result was truly in doubt.

The tally in Florida at the end of the night showed Bush with 2,909,135 votes and Gore with 2,907,351, a margin of only 1,784 votes. And, contrary to preelection predictions, Gore was ahead in the national popular vote (by a margin that would ultimately grow to half a million votes when the votes were certified), but he would lose in the Electoral College if he did not prevail in Florida.

There were other irregularities as well. Some Florida voters complained that a confusing ballot design, the "butterfly ballot," had caused them to invalidate their votes or cast votes inadvertently for Pat Buchanan instead of Al Gore. Later there would be disputes over political party involvement in absentee ballot applications, postmarks on overseas military absentee ballots, and whether some voters' names had been improperly purged from registration lists. The key issues, however, centered on how the votes would be recounted and how the final certification would occur, especially in relation to the casting of votes by presidential electors in December.

The morning after Election Day, it was clear the margin was close enough to trigger a provision in Florida law requiring an automatic machine recount. Ballots would be run through counting machines again, and the aggregation of votes from all the voting machines, precincts, and counties would be checked thoroughly. While this count took place, the campaigns anticipated later stages of the process under Florida law that governed contested elections. After the machine count, there would be a "protest" stage in which the candidates could call for recounts by hand in counties of their choosing and a "contest" phase in which a court could hear arguments about election irregularities after the votes had been certified by the secretary of state.

The automatic recount shrunk Bush's margin of victory by more than half. Gore's campaign indicated it would seek manual recounts in four counties that had voted for Gore, used a punch-card system of voting, and had a significant number of undervotes and overvotes. Undervotes are ballots that indicate no choice for the presidential race, which could occur if the voter chose to abstain from voting for president or the voter's choice was not clearly registered on the ballot. The punch-card system was particularly susceptible to undervoting, as a voter punch might not fully dislodge the chad (the rectangular piece of paper the voter must punch out) from the ballot. The Bush campaign decided not to request manual recounts in any counties.

Based on a sampling of key precincts, Palm Beach and Volusia counties agreed to proceed with the hand recounts, while Broward and Miami-Dade hesitated. On November 11, the counting began in Palm Beach. That same day, the Bush campaign filed suit in a federal district court to stop the hand recounting, arguing that the recounts in selected counties would not be conducted equally and were less accurate than machine counts.

Looming ahead of both campaigns was a deadline in Florida law for completion of the recounts seven days after Election Day. Secretary of State Katherine Harris announced that she would enforce that deadline of November 14 and that she would certify the election on November 17 when the overseas absentee ballots were received and counted. (Florida had entered a consent agreement with the Justice Department that the state would allow overseas absentee ballots to be received 10 days after an election as long as they were cast by Election Day.)

Meanwhile, the US District Court ruled against the Bush campaign, allowing the hand recounts to proceed. The counties filed suit in state court against Katherine Harris to allow the recounts to continue past the seven-day deadline and prevent her from certifying the election results until the recounts were complete. The lower state court affirmed Harris' right to enforce the deadline, but on appeal the Florida Supreme Court decided the recounts could continue past the deadline and enjoined Secretary of State Harris from certifying the election. It set a new deadline of November 26 for the results to be complete and ordered the inclusion of the hand recounts.

Hand recounts continued in several counties. The court's order was that the counties should determine the voter's intent, but no single specific standard prevailed. In the case of punch-card ballots, this spawned obscure logistical questions whose answers could determine the next president of the United States. Was a vote indicated if a chad were partially detached (how many corners detached?) or dimpled (with an indentation)? The counting was a public spectacle, with party representatives from both sides sitting behind county commissioners who scrutinized each ballot for intent, much of it covered live on television.

Despite the extension until November 26, not all counties met the deadline for counting. Some began to count and then stopped. Palm Beach County could not meet the deadline and appealed to Secretary of State Harris for a short extension. When the secretary denied the request, the county faxed partial results to her, which she did not count in the final total. At the end of this process, Gore had gained some votes, but the secretary certified results that Bush was the victor in Florida.

That evening, Florida certified the election results. Bush had 2,912,790 votes and Gore 2,912,253, a margin of 537 votes. After the certification, Gov. Jeb Bush sent a "certificate of ascertainment" to the United States archivist, with the election results and the names of the 25 Republican presidential electors who would cast their votes on December 18.

This, however, did not end the matter. Once the protest phase was complete, there were provisions in Florida law to contest the election in court. The Gore camp filed suit claiming there were several irregularities. They argued that the results of the Palm Beach recount (now complete) had been excluded; that there should have been recounts in Miami-Dade County, which had started but then stopped counting; and that the votes were counted using too strict a standard. Finally, they asked the court to retract the secretary of state's certification of the election.

During this extended counting period, Bush appealed the Florida Supreme Court decision, arguing that by extending the deadline, the Florida Supreme Court had, in effect, changed the laws that had been in place before the election and thereby undermined the legislature's power to design a method for appointing electors. The US Supreme Court issued a ruling with mixed results for both parties on December 4. It vacated the order of the Florida Supreme Court, which allowed the extension of the hand recounts, and it remanded the case to the Florida Supreme Court for a fuller explanation of its position.

At this time, the Republican-controlled Florida legislature began the process of appointing its own set of Bush electors. Republicans argued that because the Florida Supreme Court had effectively changed the election recount law with its extension of the deadline and other interpretations, the legislature had a duty to appoint its own slate of electors. The legislature, however, did not follow through on this, as the election was resolved before it acted.

The case brought by Gore proceeded to a state circuit court, which ruled against the Gore campaign. According to that court, the secretary of state had included and excluded the proper results, and the certification of the election would stand. Gore appealed to the Florida Supreme Court, which reversed the circuit court's decision. By a 4–3 vote, the Florida Supreme Court now ordered all the partial recount results included in the statewide total, ordered that counting continue in counties that had not completed their recounts, and called for a statewide recounting of undervotes. The recounts began again, with all of America and the world watching.

The counting proceeded for one afternoon. The US Supreme Court then agreed to hear an appeal by the Bush campaign. It halted the counting and asked for arguments to be presented to it on an expedited basis. Only three days later, on the night of December 12, the Court issued its opinion in the case of *Bush v. Gore* and effectively ended the election controversy.

The Court ruled 5–4 that the counting scheme as laid out by the Florida Supreme Court violated the equal protection clause of the United States Constitution. The counting scheme allowed for different methods of determining valid votes and different standards by which certain votes in certain counties would be counted. The Court also noted the state legislature's desire to have the Florida electors appointed by the December 12 "safe harbor" provision specified in federal law, and as that date was upon them, the Court argued that no timely count could go forward that satisfied equal protection concerns. The recounts would stop. The certification of George W. Bush as the victor in Florida would stand, and on December 18, the Electoral College would cast 271 electoral votes for him to Al Gore's 266 (with one abstention).

On January 6, Vice President Al Gore presided over a joint session of Congress in which the votes were counted. House members raised objections, but no senator seconded them, which would have been necessary for Congress to consider the objections. The final vote of the electors was Bush, 271, to Gore, 266 (with one Gore elector abstaining). On January 20, George W. Bush was sworn in as president of the United States.

Bush v. Gore

In the US Supreme Court case *Bush v. Gore*, the Bush team asked the Court

> whether the Florida Supreme Court established new standards
> for resolving presidential election contests, thereby violating
> Article II, section 1, clause 2 of the United States Constitution
> and failing to comply with 3 U.S.C. 5, and whether the use of
> standardless manual recounts violates Equal Protection and
> Due Process Clauses.[24]

The team's two main arguments were, first, that Florida's court had
changed the election law by changing deadlines and, second, that the
court-ordered recount would take place without uniform standards, treat-
ing votes differently.

The Court's majority opinion did not address the first argument—that
the Florida Supreme Court had effectively changed Florida election law
after the election had been held, violating the due process clause of the
Constitution and a federal law that had been passed to limit disputes over
presidential electors. According to the Constitution, state legislatures are
given plenary power to provide for the selection of electors. State legislatures may, as they have in the past, directly appoint the electors without a
popular election. But once a state legislature decides to pass a law to hold
elections, that law should be followed and not changed after the popular
election is held. If the law were subsequently changed during the counting
of the votes, it would be unfair to the voters and the candidates and would
violate the due process clause of the 14th Amendment.

In addition to the constitutional problems presented by such a change
in election law, this scenario would also run afoul of a federal law enacted
in response to the 1876 election controversy. The law, which was passed
to lessen the possibility of competing slates of electors, provides that if
a state has a law in place before Election Day and follows the provisions
of that law to resolve election disputes by six days before the presidential
electors vote, then Congress should count the slate of electors.

The real question on this point was whether the Florida Supreme Court
had changed the election law passed by the legislature. Bush and three

justices (William Rehnquist, Antonin Scalia, and Clarence Thomas) in a concurring opinion argued that changing deadlines and adopting new standards led to a new set of election laws not passed by the legislature, laws that would allow local election officials to change the election outcome by adjusting standards. Gore and the four justices in the minority (John Paul Stevens, David Souter, Ruth Bader Ginsburg, and Stephen Breyer) argued that the Florida Supreme Court was not changing the law but merely interpreting it, as was its duty, and that the law itself provided wide latitude for courts to fashion a remedy for election disputes.

The majority opinion did not take up this claim but instead focused on the narrower question of whether the Florida Supreme Court's ruling that provided for manual recounts violated the Constitution's equal protection clause. The Supreme Court ruled that the Florida Supreme Court's recounting scheme treated votes disparately because there were no uniform standards for recounting, because certain partial recounts were admitted without the certainty that full results would follow, and that the Florida court had focused on recounting undervotes, not all the ballots including overvotes. As the Court put it, "When a Court orders a statewide remedy, there must be at least some assurance that the rudimentary requirements of equal treatment and fundamental fairness are satisfied."[25] Seven justices agreed that there were equal protection problems in the recount scheme. Justices Sandra Day O'Connor, Anthony Kennedy, Thomas, and Scalia, with Chief Justice Rehnquist, believed there were constitutional problems with the recount due to a violation of the equal protection clause.

Further, they argued there was no time to recount the ballots, as both parties and the Supreme Court of Florida had indicated that Florida wished to have its electors selected by December 12—six days before they were to cast their votes—to take advantage of the "safe harbor" provision in federal law. (See Chapter 1.) Justices Breyer and Souter saw the equal protection problem but believed there was time to fashion a remedy to allow the recounts to proceed fairly.

Any recount that had continued would have had to deal with three thorny election issues. First, recounts would have surely continued beyond the December 12 "safe harbor" deadline. It is even conceivable that a statewide hand recount with potential judicial challenges would have gone on beyond December 18, when the electors were to cast their votes. Second, continuing the recounts might have led to competing slates of electors. Third, an extended dispute might have continued into January, when the Congress would count the electoral votes, and might have ended up unresolved by Inauguration Day. Let us examine each issue in turn.

What If the Count Had Continued Beyond December 12, 2000?

A federal law calls for the appointment of a slate of electors to be "conclusive" if a state has provided by law for election controversies to be resolved at least six days before the presidential electors cast their votes. If recounts in 2000 had continued past December 12, this "safe harbor" would not have been met.

The "safe harbor" comes into play when Congress is to count the votes. If Congress has before it one slate of electors appointed according to state law at least six days before the date when the electors' votes were cast, the law requires this appointment to be conclusive. But Congress still has some latitude in judging whether these votes were "regularly given" and whether the state law for resolving controversies has been followed. One might imagine a case in which Congress objects to a slate of electors submitted before the "safe harbor" deadline if it finds other irregularities. Nevertheless, despite Congress' power to count the votes of the presidential electors, the "safe harbor" provision is significant, one that both parties to *Bush v. Gore* and the Florida Supreme Court regarded as the date by which Florida should appoint its electors.

Electors appointed after the "safe harbor" date are subject to greater challenge, but it is still up to Congress to decide whether to count the electors. There is even the precedent of the 1960 election. Hawaii submitted a slate of electors for Richard Nixon in mid-December, but when a recount showed John F. Kennedy to be the winner, Hawaii submitted a new set for Kennedy in January after the electors had cast their votes. In this case, Congress counted the later slate rather than the earlier one.

Ultimately, Congress counts the votes. The federal law governs certain scenarios, but Congress has latitude in interpreting how the law applies to a particular election dispute.

What If There Had Been Competing Slates of Electors?

The circumstances of the 2000 election brought about a situation in which, conceivably, Congress could have been presented with more than one slate of Florida electors. When Secretary of State Harris certified the election, the governor appointed a slate of electors for Bush based on that certification. If the counting had continued as the Florida Supreme Court had ordered, and if Gore had gone ahead in the recounts, the Florida Supreme Court might have appointed or ordered the appointment of a slate of Gore electors. Also, the state legislature was poised to appoint a set of Bush electors when the Supreme Court decided *Bush v. Gore*.

Federal law does have something to say about competing electors. A slate of electors appointed according to a preexisting state law that provides for resolution of election contests by six days before the voting of the Electoral College would be "conclusive" if there were no other slate of electors. But a second set of electors appointed after the "safe harbor" period would cast doubt as to whether the election had been resolved by the earlier date. Ultimately, two slates of electors would be presented to Congress, which would entertain objections and try to resolve them. If Congress could not agree, federal law would give preference to the slate appointed by the governor. But if the recount had shown a Gore victory, the Florida courts might have compelled the governor to submit a second slate of electors pledged to Gore. In this case, federal law would not have given guidance as to how Congress was to proceed.

The 107th Congress that took office on January 3, 2001, was split. Republicans controlled the House, but the Senate was equally divided. The tie was broken by the vice president—none other than Al Gore, whose term would expire on January 20. Democrats effectively controlled the Senate. With split control of the two houses, a dispute over a set of electors that could not be resolved under the federal law might have resulted in a deadlock that continued to Inauguration Day.

What If the Election Dispute Had Extended to Inauguration Day?

The Hayes-Tilden election of 1876 was resolved only two days before Inauguration Day. If a deadlock in Congress over counting the votes had arisen in Congress in 2001, there might have been no resolution by January 20, when the 43rd president of the United States was to take office.

If this had occurred, Republican Speaker Dennis Hastert would have acted as president of the United States, provided he resigned his House seat and Speakership. Hastert would have served the four years of the term, unless the Congress subsequently resolved the election dispute and elected a president or a vice president, in which case Hastert would have been displaced. If Hastert had chosen not to act as president, the president pro tempore of the Senate, Sen. Robert Byrd (D-WV) would have been next in line. (The 99-year-old Strom Thurmond had been president pro tempore in the previous Congress and resumed that position for a time when George W. Bush became president and the Senate changed back to Republican hands.)

If Byrd had declined, the line of succession would have proceeded to the Clinton cabinet. Secretary of State Madeleine Albright was ineligible to serve as president, as she was foreign-born. Secretary of Treasury Larry Summers was next in line, followed by the other heads of departments in order of the creation of those departments.

Conclusion

The 2000 election was an extraordinary event. It had been over 100 years since the winner of the popular vote did not also win a majority in the Electoral College, although only 16 years later, the popular vote and Electoral College vote diverged again.

This section has illustrated that there are two types of elections that might be controversial under the Electoral College system: multicandidate elections, in which no one receives a majority of the Electoral College, and extremely close elections. Neither is likely. The Electoral College and other features of our politics encourage a two-party system and make the 1824 scenario remote. As for extremely close elections, it is true that we are in a period of parity between the parties, with the presidency, Congress, and control of state governments up for grabs for Democrats and Republicans. However, even this close competition is unlikely to result in a dead heat in a single state, whose outcome would determine the winner of a majority of the Electoral College.

The parallel to 2000 is the 1876 election, in which disputes over results in several states, including Florida, led to a dispute over which slate of electors should be counted by Congress. But in several ways the 1876 election was more divisive. First, the election controversy dragged on much longer. The dispute continued past the time that the electors cast their votes; past the date when Congress was to count the votes, as legislators could not agree on which electoral slates to count; and to within two days of Inauguration Day, which at that time was in March. Second, the dispute over slates of electors was in several cases a dispute over rival governments in the Reconstruction-era South. It was not merely a case of close margins in the popular votes, but of rival groups, each claiming corruption on the part of the others, submitting slates of electors. Finally, while the 2000 dispute was limited to Florida, in 1876 there were disputes over the slates of electors from a number of states.

The 2000 election was hotly contested, but it was resolved before the presidential electors cast their votes. With hindsight, Gore would have had a difficult time prevailing under many scenarios if the election dispute had extended into January because Republicans controlled the House of Representatives, commanding a majority of the seats and the state delegations and holding the Speakership. If the dispute had continued and the Democrats had been willing to settle for Republican Dennis Hastert instead, they might have been able to deny Bush the presidency, but they would have had to overcome significant political hurdles to elect Gore.

In the current polarized competitive environment, in which state legislatures, secretaries of state, governors, and federal and state courts may favor one party or the other, the 2000 election highlights the problems we may see in coming years. Arguments over the counting and recounting of ballots, the role of state legislatures, the tight time frame for resolving recounts, and ultimately Congress' role in counting the electoral votes might amplify already tense political conflict. Also relevant to today is that a delay in resolving an election would increase tension and confusion and raise questions of whether we can meet an important deadline for electors casting ballots. Fortunately, one aspect of the 2000 election makes it unlikely to be a regular paradigm for elections: that the election came down to one state where the parties were separated by a few hundred votes.

.

Part III

Arguments for and Against the Electoral College

10

Let's Hear It for the Electoral College

Walter Berns

On January 8, 1981, following the election in which John Anderson ran as an independent candidate, I began a *Wall Street Journal* article titled "Let's Hear It for the Electoral College" by pointing out that "where the Electoral College is concerned, nothing fails to succeed like success."[26] By success, I meant that the Electoral College regularly produces a president with a clear and immediate claim to the office, in part because it exaggerates the margin of victory in the popular vote. It did this in 1980 and, until 2000, in every subsequent election, but this did not satisfy its critics, some of whom have made a career of proposing constitutional amendments abolishing the Electoral College.[27]

Their complaints are familiar. The Electoral College, we are told, is a "relic," an "absurdly dangerous" method of selecting a president that threatens to "plunge the nation into political chaos." The presumed danger is that a candidate might receive a majority of the electoral votes while receiving fewer popular votes than his or her opponent.

The critics speak of the popular versus electoral vote discrepancy as a "time bomb waiting to go off," but the last time it did go off, in 1888, nothing happened. There was hardly a ripple of popular discontent, no spate of editorials claiming that Benjamin Harrison was an illegitimate president, no complaints from the losing candidate, Grover Cleveland, that he had been cheated. Indeed, when asked by a reporter the day after the election to what he attributed his defeat, Cleveland smiled and said, "It was mainly because the other party got more votes."[28]

It was different in 2000. No sooner had the election results been reported when Al Gore's campaign chairman claimed fraud and Sen. Hillary Rodham Clinton (and even the Republican Sen. Arlen Specter) said the Electoral College had to be abolished in favor of a direct popular vote.

Have we really reached the point where the right to hold an office depends *solely* on the suffrage of a popular majority? Are the sponsors of the proposed constitutional amendments willing to say that a candidate elected with a *constitutional* but not a popular majority is an illegitimate president? Perhaps, but only if the moral authority of the Electoral College—indeed, of the Constitution itself—has been undermined by the persistent efforts to get rid of it, especially those of members of Congress and what the British call the "chattering class."

The Electoral College is said to be undemocratic, a violation of the democratic principles of majority rule and one man, one vote. In fact, however, the majority now rules, but it does so at the state level where (except in Maine and Nebraska) the votes are aggregated. As it happens, this is where the vote of any particular minority looms larger, or carries more weight, than it is likely to do in the country as a whole.

As long as a minority is not distributed evenly throughout the country, it is in its interest to oppose direct popular elections; civil rights leaders used to understand this. And is there not something to be said for an electoral system that threatens to penalize a political party and its candidate for failing to respect the rights of respectable minorities? Furthermore, is there not something to be said for an electoral system that protects the interests of states as states, which is to say, a system with an element of federalism built into it? Only twice in this century (1960 and 1976) has the candidate with an Electoral College majority failed to win a majority of the states. And is there not, then, something to be said for a system that threatens to penalize sectional candidates?

The American idea of democracy cannot be expressed in the simple but insidious formula of the greatest good for the greatest number. What the greatest number regards as its greatest good might very well prove to be a curse to those who are not part of that number. The American idea of democracy, which is expressed in the Declaration of Independence and embodied in various provisions of the Constitution, is that government is instituted to secure the rights of all. What is constitutionalism if not a qualification of majoritarianism?

The men who founded this country surely recognized the entitlements of a popular majority, but, with an eye to the qualifications or qualities required of an office, they devised institutions, such as the Electoral

College, to modify or qualify the majority principle. Nothing could be clearer than that the founders sought institutions or ways—Alexis de Tocqueville called them "forms"—to protect the country from what has come to be called populism. The Senate's organizing principle is surely not majority rule, nor are its procedures simply democratic. Federal judges are not elected at all.

If legitimacy springs only from the principle of one man, one equally weighted vote, upon what meat do these our judicial Caesars feed? If populism is our only principle, why should the people vote? Why not select all public officials by lot? This would be truly democratic, because it pays no attention whatsoever to the qualifications of officeholders—or assumes that everyone is equally qualified.

In short, the issue that ought to engage our attention is the one the framers debated over the entire course of the Constitutional Convention—namely, what system is more likely to produce a president with the qualities required of the person who holds this great office? In all the years I have been engaged with this issue, I have yet to encounter a critic of the Electoral College who argues that a president chosen directly by the people is likely to be a better president.

My argument was best made by the late Professor Herbert Storing when he testified before the Subcommittee on the Constitution of the Senate Judiciary Committee (on July 27, 1977). He said:

> To see the case for the present system of electing the president requires a shift in point of view from that usually taken by the critics [of the Electoral College]. They tend to view elections in terms of *input*—in terms of the right to vote, equal weight of votes, who in fact votes, and the like. The framers [of the Constitution] thought it at least as important to consider the *output* of any given electoral system. What kind of men does it bring to office? How will it affect the working of the political system? What is its bearing on the political character of the whole country?

If James Madison, Alexander Hamilton, James Wilson, Benjamin Franklin, Gouverneur Morris, and the rest thought it important to consider *output* and *input* when designing the electoral system, I think that we today are obliged to do the same when considering proposals to amend it.

11

Why Old and New Arguments for the Electoral College Are Not Compelling

Akhil Reed Amar and Vikram David Amar

Looking back at the odd election of 2000, it is hard not to fixate on Florida and the courts.[29] But these absorbing soap operas should not obscure the other historical headline: The national popular vote loser nonetheless won the Electoral College vote. Does this represent a flaw in our Constitution? Should we scrap the Electoral College in favor of direct popular vote? Practically speaking, can we do so?

Our analysis proceeds in two parts. First, we will critique standard historical accounts of, and justifications for, the Electoral College. Second, we will consider prominent modern arguments on behalf of the current system. We are advocates of an alternative to the Electoral College— instant runoff voting, which we believe is the best method for conducting a direct popular vote—but in this piece, we will stick to discussing our objections to the Electoral College.

Original Arguments for the Electoral College

Let's begin by considering why the Philadelphia framers invented an intricate Electoral College contraption in the first place and why, after its gears jammed in the Adams-Jefferson-Burr election of 1800–01, the 12th Amendment repaired the thing rather than junking it. Why didn't early Americans simply opt for direct national election of the president? The typical answers taught in grade school civics miss much of the real story, both by misreading the evidence from Philadelphia and by ignoring the significance of later events, especially the 12th Amendment.

The Electoral College Does Not Really Help Small States—Nor Was It Designed to. It is often said that the founders chose the Electoral College over direct election to balance the interests of big (high-population) and small (low-population) states. The key Philadelphia concession to small states was the framers' backup selection system: If no candidate emerged with a first-round electoral vote majority, then the House of Representatives would choose among the top five finalists, with each state casting one vote, regardless of population. According to the standard story, although big states would predictably dominate the first round, small states could expect to loom large in the final selection.

But, as James Madison insisted,[30] the deepest political divisions in early America were not between big and small states as such; rather, the real fissures separated North from South and East from West. Moreover, once the modern system of national presidential parties and winner-takes-all state contests emerged—a system already visible, though not yet entrenched, at the time of the 12th Amendment—the big states obviously had the advantage.

With two national presidential parties, one candidate almost always had an electoral majority in the first round, rendering irrelevant the framers' backup system favoring small states. (Three or four strong candidates, in contrast, might have split the vote so that no one garnered a majority.) And winner-takes-all rules—under which a candidate who won a state got all its electoral votes, not a number proportional to the extent of his or her win—compounded the advantage of big states.

Indeed, before the Civil War amendments (which changed the Electoral College yet again), only two of the 16 presidents hailed from small states—Louisiana's Zachary Taylor and New Hampshire's Franklin Pierce. And of the 26 men to hold the office since the Civil War, only Bill Clinton of Arkansas claimed residence in a small state.

In sum, if the framers' chief goal was to give small states a leg up, they did a rather bad job of it. (We shall suggest below, however, that their true goal was something different.)

How the Founders' Concern About Voter Information Was Rendered Obsolete. Another founding-era argument for the Electoral College stemmed from the objection to direct election that ordinary Americans across a vast continent would lack sufficient information to choose intelligently among leading presidential candidates.

This objection is sometimes described today as reflecting a general distrust of democracy among the founders. But that is not quite right; after all, the framers required that the House be directly elected every two years, sharply breaking with the indirect election of congressmen under the Articles of Confederation. Many leading Federalists also supported direct election of governors.

The key objection at Philadelphia was thus not to democracy per se, but to democracy based on inadequate voter information. The founders believed that although voters in a given state would know enough to choose among leading state candidates for House races and the governorship, they would likely lack information about which out-of-state figure would be best for the presidency.

This objection rang true in the 1780s, when life was far more local. But the early emergence of national presidential parties rendered the objection obsolete by linking presidential candidates to slates of local candidates and national platforms that explained to voters who stood for what.

The 1800–01 Election and the 12th Amendment's Transformation of the Electoral College. Although the Philadelphia framers did not anticipate the rise of national presidential parties, the 12th Amendment (proposed in 1803 and ratified a year later) was framed with such parties in mind in the aftermath of the election of 1800–01. In that election, two rudimentary presidential parties—Federalists led by John Adams and Democratic-Republicans led by Thomas Jefferson—took shape and squared off. Jefferson ultimately prevailed, but only after an extended crisis triggered by several glitches in the framers' electoral machinery. In particular, Democratic-Republican electors had no formal way to designate that they wanted Jefferson for president and Aaron Burr for vice president rather than vice versa. Some politicians then tried to exploit the resulting confusion.

Enter the 12th Amendment, which allowed each party to designate one candidate for president and a separate candidate for vice president. The amendment transformed the framers' framework, enabling subsequent presidential elections to be openly populist and partisan affairs featuring two competing tickets. It is the 12th Amendment's Electoral College system, not the Philadelphia framers', that remains in place today. Yet the amendment typically goes unmentioned in standard civics accounts of the Constitution.

The election of 1800–01 also helped allay another early anxiety about a popularly elected president. At the founding, some saw a populist presidency as uniquely dangerous—inviting demagoguery and possibly dictatorship, with one man claiming to embody the voice of the American people. The dictator/demagogue concern was greater for a president than a governor, given the president's broader electoral mandate and status as continental commander in chief. But with Jefferson's election, Americans began to embrace a system in which presidential aspirants ran national campaigns, sought direct voter approval, and claimed popular mandates upon election.

The Key Role of Slavery in the History of the Electoral College. The biggest flaw in standard civics accounts of the Electoral College is that they never mention the real demon dooming direct national election in 1787 and 1803: slavery.

At the Philadelphia convention, the visionary Pennsylvanian James Wilson proposed direct national election of the president.[31] But in a key speech on July 19, the savvy Virginian James Madison suggested that such a system would prove unacceptable to the South: "The right of suffrage was much more diffusive in the Northern than the Southern States; and the latter could have no influence in the election on the score of Negroes."[32]

In other words, in a direct election system, the North would outnumber the South, whose many slaves (more than half a million in all) of course could not vote. But the Electoral College—a prototype of which Madison proposed in this same speech—instead let each southern state count its slaves, albeit with a two-fifths discount, in computing its share of the overall Electoral College.

Virginia emerged as the big winner—the California of the founding era—with 12 out of a total of 91 electors allocated by the Philadelphia Constitution, more than a quarter of the 46 needed to win in the first round. After the 1800 census, Wilson's free state of Pennsylvania had 10 percent more free persons than Virginia but received 20 percent fewer electoral votes. Perversely, the more slaves Virginia (or any other slave state) bought or bred, the more electoral votes it would receive. Were a slave state to free any blacks who then moved to the North, the state could actually lose electoral votes.

If the system's proslavery tilt was not overwhelmingly obvious when the Constitution was ratified, it quickly became so. For 32 of the Constitution's first 36 years, a white slaveholding Virginian occupied the presidency.

Southerner Thomas Jefferson, for example, won the election of 1800–01 against northerner John Adams in a race in which the slavery skew of the Electoral College was the decisive margin of victory: Without the extra Electoral College votes generated by slavery, the mostly southern states that supported Jefferson would not have sufficed to give him a majority. As observers pointedly remarked at the time, Thomas Jefferson metaphorically rode into the executive mansion on the backs of slaves.

The 1796 contest between Adams and Jefferson had featured an even sharper division between northern and southern states. Thus, when the 12th Amendment tinkered with the Electoral College system rather than tossing it, the system's proslavery bias was hardly a secret. Indeed, in the floor debate over the amendment in late 1803, Massachusetts Congressman Samuel Thatcher complained that "the representation of slaves adds thirteen members to this House in the present Congress, and eighteen Electors of President and Vice President at the next election."[33] But Thatcher's complaint went unredressed. Once again, the North caved to the South by refusing to insist on direct national election.

How the Electoral College Also Hurt Women's Suffrage. The Founding Fathers' Electoral College also did not do much for the Founding Mothers. In a system of direct national election, any state that chose to enfranchise its women would have automatically doubled its clout in presidential elections. (New Jersey apparently did allow some women to vote in the founding era but later abandoned the practice.) Under the Electoral College, however, a state had no special incentive to expand suffrage; each state received a fixed number of electoral votes based on population, regardless of how many or how few citizens were allowed to vote or actually voted. As with slaves, what mattered was simply how many women resided in a state, not how many could vote there.

Modern Arguments for the Electoral College

In light of this more complete (if less flattering) account of the Electoral College in the late 18th and early 19th centuries, Americans must ask themselves whether we want to maintain this peculiar institution in the 21st century. Most millennial Americans no longer believe in slavery or sexism. We do not believe that voters lack proper information about national candidates. We do not believe that a national figure claiming a national mandate is unacceptably dangerous. What we do believe is that each American is an equal citizen. We celebrate the idea of one person, one vote—an idea the Electoral College undermines.

Of course, a system with dirty roots could nevertheless make sense today for rather different reasons than the ones present at the creation. Having considered the original arguments for the Electoral College, we now offer a critique of the top 10 modern arguments for the Electoral College.

Number 1: The Argument from Political Interest. Some might prefer the Electoral College because it advantages a given political interest—say, rural voters or racial minorities. But does today's Electoral College systematically favor any given faction? Not likely.

True, the Electoral College was designed to and did in fact advantage southern, white, male, propertied slaveholders in the antebellum era. And in the election of 2000, it again ended up working against women, blacks, and the poor, who voted overwhelmingly for Gore. But it is just as easy to imagine an alternative scenario in which Gore won the electoral vote while losing the national popular vote. Indeed, most pundits going into Election Day thought this the more likely scenario.

Analytically, the Electoral College privileges small states by giving every state three electoral votes at the start. This tends to help Republicans, who win among rural whites. But the college also exaggerates the power of big states, via winner-takes-all rules. That tends to help Democrats, who win among urban minorities.

In today's world, the two opposing skews largely cancel each other out. Republicans often win more states overall, but Democrats often win more big states. The net effect is to add to the political deck a pair of jokers—one red and one blue—which randomly surface to mock the equality idea by giving the prize to the candidate who lost the national popular vote.

In any event, even assuming the Electoral College systemically helps some interest group, this is hardly a principled argument in its favor. Our Constitution should not rig elections to favor any particular faction or party. We should treat all presidential voters equally, just as we do gubernatorial voters in states.

Number 2: The Tennis Analogy. Electoral College defenders sometimes compare the electoral process with tennis. A tennis player, they say, can win more points overall, and even more games than an opponent, yet still lose the match. So, too, with many other sports; for example, a baseball team might get more hits or win more innings but still lose the game.

So what is the problem if something similar happens with the Electoral College?

The problem is that elections are not sporting events. It matters who wins, and the objective is not simply to make the thing exciting or random. All tennis points are not created equal, but all American citizens are. To talk of tennis is simply to sidestep rather than engage the moral principle favoring one man, one vote.

The tennis trope is a silly analogy, not a serious argument. It also proves too much, calling into question our standard mode of picking state governors. Ditto for a variant of the tennis analogy, which casually dismisses direct popular election as simpleminded majoritarianism.

Number 3: The Media Argument. Its defenders argue that without the Electoral College, candidates will spend all their time trying to rack up big victories in big cities with big media, ignoring the rest of the voters.

But this objection also proves too much. The same thing might be said of the California governor's election. And the Electoral College itself often focuses candidates narrowly on a few swing locations to the detriment of most other regions.

Number 4: The Geographic Concentration Argument. Defenders also contend that the Electoral College prevents purely regional candidates from winning by requiring the winner to put together a continental coalition popular in many different regions.

Really? Then how did Lincoln win the Electoral College without winning a single southern state—indeed, without winning a single vote south of Virginia? Didn't the elections of 1796 and 1800 also feature sharp sectional divisions between North and South? Moreover, if geographic spread is a good argument for a continental Electoral College, why isn't it an equally good argument for an intrastate Electoral College for vast and populous states like California and Texas?

Under direct election, presidential candidates would continue to wage broad national campaigns appealing to voters in different states and regions; one simply cannot reach 50 percent without getting lots of votes in lots of places.

Number 5: The Argument from Inertia. Some supporters of the Electoral College have argued that a change in presidential selection rules would radically alter the election game: Because candidates would no longer care about winning states—only votes—campaign strategies would change dramatically and for the worse.

It is hard to see why, given that, historically, the Electoral College leader has also tended to be the popular vote leader. Granted, had direct election been in place in 2000, the candidates might have run slightly different campaigns. For example, Bush might have tried to rack up even more votes in his home state, while Gore might have avoided bad-mouthing it ("messing with Texas"). But these likely changes of strategy would have been neither big nor bad.

Again, why would a system that works so well for state governors fail for the presidency?

Number 6: The Senate Anxiety. The claim that the principle of one person, one vote would likewise doom the equal representation of states in the United States Senate at least raises a fair point. The equality idea that favors the abolition of the Electoral College does raise questions about Senate malapportionment. Why should the almost 40 million citizens living in California get no more senators than the half-million citizens living in Wyoming?

But the Electoral College issue is nevertheless distinguishable. On Election Day, Americans vote in 33 (or 34) separate Senate races, each featuring a different candidate matchup. These votes cannot simply be added together. To try to add them up—x percent for "the Democrat" and y percent for "the Republican"—is artificial in the extreme, given that 33 different Democrats are running against 33 different Republicans in 33 different races.

In contrast, presidential votes can be aggregated across America. Indeed, it is artificial not to add them together, and the violation of equality is much more flagrant when a person who plainly got fewer votes is nevertheless named the winner.

Number 7: The Third-Party and Plurality Winner Problem. Some defenders of the Electoral College worry that direct election either could lead to a low-plurality winner (say, with 35 percent of the vote) in a three- or four-way race or would require a high cutoff (say, 45 percent) that would require a runoff. Allowing runoffs would encourage third-party spoilers.

But the same thing is true for states, which manage to elect governors just fine. Moreover, a low-plurality winner in a three- or four-way race is possible even with the Electoral College (which has also attracted its fair share of spoilers—just ask Ross Perot or Ralph Nader).

Finally, the problem could easily be solved in a direct national election by a system called single-transferable voting, in which voters list their second and third choices on the ballot—in effect, combining the first heat and runoff elections into a single "instant runoff" transaction.

Number 8: The Recount Nightmare. Other Electoral College fans are haunted by the specter of recounts: "If you thought the recount in Florida was a disaster, can you imagine the nightmare of a national recount?"

But if California, Texas, New York, and other large states can handle recounts for governors' races, a national recount should likewise be manageable, especially with new technology that will make counting and recounting easier in the future. Fair vote counts and sensible recounts are simply part and parcel of a basic system of one person, one vote.

Moreover, the Electoral College does not avoid, and at times can worsen, the recount nightmare: A razor-thin Electoral College margin may require recounts in a number of closely contested states even if there is a clear national popular winner. But the recount issue does remind us that direct national election would ideally involve uniform national standards for counting and recounting votes.

Number 9: The Modern Federalism Argument. Many supporters of the Electoral College parade under the banners of "federalism" and "states' rights." But direct national election would give state governments a better role than they now enjoy.

Under direct election, each state government would have some incentive to make it easier for its citizens to vote—say, by making Election Day a holiday or by providing paid time off—because the more state voters who turn out, the bigger the states' overall share in the national tally. Direct national election would thus encourage states to innovate and compete to increase turnout and improve democracy.

Of course, national oversight would be appropriate to keep the innovation and competition within proper bounds—no deceased or infant voters, please! Presidential elections would thus continue to reflect a mix of federal and state laws and respect proper state innovation within a federal framework—in short, federalism at its best.

Number 10: The Futility Argument. A final argument against reform sounds realpolitik: Adopting direct popular election would require a constitutional amendment, and no such amendment is likely, given the high hurdles set out in Article V—two-thirds of the Congress and three-quarters of the states.

But the premise of this argument is wrong. Much as early 20th-century Americans improvised systems of direct election of senators before the 17th Amendment, so 21st-century Americans could improvise systems of direct presidential election without the need of a formal constitutional amendment. (We will not go into the details here; interested readers should consult our online FindLaw column of December 28, 2001.[34])

More generally, the futility argument is hardly a principled defense of the Electoral College, and principle matters. If the Electoral College is the right principle, shouldn't other nations adopt it for their own presidencies? (They haven't.) Shouldn't states adopt an Electoral College look-alike for their governorships? (Again, they haven't.) Conversely, if direct election truly makes sense—in both practice and principle—for the chief executive of California, New York, Texas, and every other state, why not for the chief executive of all the states?

12

Excerpts from *The Electoral College and the American Idea of Democracy*

Martin Diamond

Why the Framers Adopted the Electoral College

The device of independent electors as a substitute for direct popular election was hit upon for three reasons, none of which supports the thesis that the intention was fundamentally undemocratic.[35] First and above all, the electors were not devised as an undemocratic substitute for the popular will, but rather as a nationalizing substitute for the state legislatures. In short, the Electoral College, like so much else in the Constitution, was the product of the give-and-take and the compromises between the large and the small states, or more precisely, between the confederalists—those who sought to retain much of the Articles of Confederation—and those who advocated a large, primarily national republic.

It will be remembered that there was a great struggle at the Constitutional Convention over this issue, which was the matrix out of which many of the main constitutional provisions emerged. As they did regarding the House of Representatives and the Senate, the confederalists fought hard to have the president selected by the state legislatures or by some means that retained the primacy of the states as states. It was to fend off this confederalizing threat that the leading framers, James Madison, James Wilson, and Gouverneur Morris, hit upon the Electoral College device. As a matter of fact, their own first choice was for a straight national popular vote; Wilson introduced that idea, and Madison and Morris endorsed it.[36] But when the "states' righters" vehemently rejected it, Wilson, Madison, and Morris settled on the device of popularly elected electors. The Electoral College, thus, in its genesis and inspiration, was not an antidemocratic but an anti–states' rights device, a way of keeping the election from state politicians and giving it to the people.[37]

Second, the system of electors also had to be devised because most of the delegates to the Convention feared not democracy itself but only that a straightforward national election was "impracticable" in a country as large as the United States, given the poor internal communications it then had.[38] Many reasonably feared that, in these circumstances, the people simply could not have the national information about available candidates to make any real choice, let alone an intelligent one. And small-state partisans feared that, given this lack of information, ordinary voters would vote for favorite sons, with the result that large-state candidates would always win the presidential pluralities.[39]

How seriously concerned the framers were with this "communications gap" is shown by the famous faulty mechanism in the original provisions (the one that made possible the Jefferson-Burr deadlock in 1801). Each elector was originally to cast two votes, but without specifying which was for president and which for vice president. The Constitution required that at least one of these two votes be for a non-home-state candidate, the intention being to force the people and their electors to cast at least one electoral vote for a truly "continental" figure. Clearly, then, what the framers were seeking was not an undemocratic way to substitute elite electors for the popular will; rather, as they claimed, they were trying to find a practicable way to extract from the popular will a non-parochial choice for the president.

The third reason for the electoral scheme likewise had nothing to do with frustrating democracy, but rather with the wide variety of suffrage practices in the states. Madison dealt with this problem at the Constitutional Convention on July 19, 1787. While election by "the people was in his opinion the fittest in itself," there was a serious circumstantial difficulty: "The right of suffrage was much more diffusive in the Northern than the Southern states; and the latter could have no influence in the election on the score of the Negroes. The substitution of electors obviated this difficulty."[40] That is, the Electoral College would take care of the discrepancies between the voting population and the total population of the states until, as Madison hoped and expected, slavery would be eliminated and suffrage discrepancies would gradually disappear. Again, the intention was to find the most practical means in the circumstances to secure a popular choice of the president.

Why the Electoral College Is Democratic (Through the States)

In fact, presidential elections are already just about as democratic as they can be. We already have one man, one vote—*but in the states*. Elections are as freely and democratically contested as elections can be—*but in the states*. Victory always goes democratically to the winner of the raw popular vote—*but in the states*. The label given to the proposed reform—"direct popular election"—is a misnomer; the elections have already become as directly popular as they can be—*but in the states*. Despite all their democratic rhetoric, the reformers do not propose to make our presidential elections more directly democratic; they only propose to make them more directly national, by entirely removing the states from the electoral process. Democracy thus is not the question regarding the Electoral College; federalism is. Should our presidential elections remain in part *federally* democratic, or should we make them completely *nationally* democratic?

Whatever we decide, then, democracy itself is not at stake in our decision, only the prudential question of how to channel and organize the popular will. That makes everything easier. When the question is only whether the federally democratic aspect of the Electoral College should be abandoned to prevent the remotely possible election of a president who has not won the national popular vote, it does not seem so hard to opt for retaining some federalism in this homogenizing, centralizing age. When federalism has already been weakened, perhaps inevitably in modern circumstances, why further weaken the federal elements in our political system by destroying the informal federal element that has historically evolved in our system of presidential elections?

The crucial general-ticket system, adopted in the 1830s for reasons pertinent then, has become in our time a constitutionally unplanned but vital support for federalism. Also called the "unit rule" system, it provides that the state's entire electoral vote goes to the winner of the popular vote in the state. Resting entirely on the voluntary legislative action of each state, this informal historical development, combined with the formal constitutional provision, has generated a federal element in the Electoral College that sends a federalizing impulse throughout our whole political process. It makes the states as states dramatically and pervasively import-ant in the whole presidential nominating process, from the earliest stages in the nominating campaign through the convention and final election. De-federalize the presidential election—which is what direct popular elec-tion boils down to—and a contrary nationalizing impulse will gradually work its way throughout the political process. The nominating process naturally takes its cues from the electing process; the same cuing process would continue, but in reverse.[41]

It is hard to think of a worse time than the present, when so much already tends toward excessive centralization, to strike an unnecessary blow at the federal quality of our political order. The federal aspect of the electoral controversy has received inadequate attention; indeed, it is regarded by many as irrelevant to it. The argument has been that the president is the representative of "all the people" and, hence, that he should be elected by them in a wholly national way, unimpeded by the interposition of the states. Unfortunately, the prevailing conception of federalism encourages this erroneous view. We tend nowadays to have a narrowed conception of federalism, limiting it to the reserved powers of the states.

But by focusing exclusively on the division of power between the states and the central government, we overlook an equally vital aspect of federalism—namely, the federal elements in the central government itself. The Senate (which, after all, helps make laws for all the people) is the most obvious example; it is organized on the federal principle of equal representation of each state. Even the House of Representatives has federal elements in its design and mode of operation. There is no reason, then, why the president, admittedly the representative of all of us, cannot represent us and hence be elected by us in a way correspond-ing to our compoundly federal and national character. The American Bar Association report of 1967, for example, begs the question when it says that "it seems most appropriate that the election of the nation's only two national officers be by national referendum."[42] They are our two *central* officers. But they are not our two *national* officers; under the Constitution, they are our two *partly federal, partly national* officers. Why should we wish to change them into our two wholly *national* officers?

13

Public Opinion on the Electoral College

Karlyn Bowman

In 1944, the Gallup Organization asked what appears to be the first question in the public opinion literature about the Electoral College.[43] People were asked in in-person interviews what the "Electoral College vote system" was, and 54 percent said they did not know or did not understand it. Another 8 percent gave vague or incomplete answers, 3 percent incorrect ones, and 2 percent "probably incorrect" responses. Around 18 percent gave partially correct responses. Only 16 percent answered directly that it was an indirect method of electing the president.

In 10 surveys between 1947 and 1961, more than 45 percent gave either an incorrect answer or some version of a "don't know" or "no answer" response to Gallup's interviewers' questions about the Electoral College. Comparing the results of these knowledge questions directly is not possible because the interviewers categorized the responses differently. Suffice it to say, many Americans were not familiar with the Electoral College.

More recent questions about *knowledge* of the Electoral College are sparse in the polling literature. Shortly after the 2000 election, 30 percent told Gallup they understood the Electoral College system very well, 42 percent somewhat well, 18 percent not too well, and 10 percent not at all. In a 2018 Pew Research Center question, people were asked to choose among four responses to describe the Electoral College. Seventy-six percent chose the correct answer, "an assembly that formally elects the president," while smaller numbers said the Electoral College supervises the presidential debates (7 percent), is another name for the US Congress (6 percent), and trains those who run for political office (5 percent).

Taken together, these questions about people's knowledge asked in polls over three-quarters of a century might suggest that Americans do not have firm opinions about the Electoral College. But as we will see, that is not the case. Americans' opinions on the questions available to us are clear and consistent. In virtually every question pollsters have asked, Americans favor direct election of the president.

*

Early Polls on the Electoral College

Most polling organizations flit from one subject to another, usually depending on what is in the news. In many areas, trends about Americans' opinions are nonexistent. Only two polling organizations, Gallup and CBS News, have over-time data with virtually identical questions on people's view of the Electoral College.

Gallup's first question asking people their opinion of (as opposed to their knowledge of) the Electoral College was asked in 1948. Of those people who had some idea of what the Electoral College was (52 percent of the sample), 31 percent said it should be continued, while 56 percent said it should not. Another question asked of those with some awareness of what the Electoral College was (42 percent of those sampled) asked people whether it served "any real purpose," to which 31 percent answered yes and 58 percent no.

From 1948 to 1965, people were asked about the system of electing presidents, although the words "Electoral College" were not used (Table 1). The responses move within a narrow range, with half or more in each question indicating that the system should be changed. The "no opinion" responses ranged from a low of 13 percent in December 1960 to a high of 27 percent in the first question from 1948.

The next question came in 1967 after President Lyndon Johnson called for eliminating the Electoral College in a January 1966 Special Message to Congress. In the message, the president called for a constitutional amendment to provide four-year terms for members of the House of Representatives and, separately, reform of the Electoral College. The president cited what he saw as "defects" in the system of electing the president and called for their elimination "in order to assure that the

Table 1. Polls on the Electoral College, 1948–65

Q: *Today, the presidential candidate who gets the most popular votes in a state takes all the electoral votes of that state. Do you think this should or should not be changed so that each of the candidates would receive the same proportion of electoral votes that he gets in the popular vote? This would mean, for example, that if a candidate gets two-thirds of the popular vote in a state, he would then get two-thirds of the electoral votes of that state.*

	System should be changed so that each of the candidates would receive the same proportion of electoral votes that he gets in the popular vote	System should not be changed
1948*	63%	16%
1948	58	15
1950	57	22
1951	57	21
1954 (December 1954–January 1955)	51	28
1955 (November)	58	27
1960 (March)	50	28
1960 (December)	59	27
1961	61	21
1965	57	28

Note: In this question, Gallup coded a response "qualified should" at 1 percent. The question from 1951 has slightly different wording.
Source: Gallup Organization, latest that of 1965.

people's will shall not be frustrated in the choice of their President and Vice President."[44]

Among the defects President Johnson articulated were (1) the risk of unpledged electors being manipulated to undermine the election of a major party candidate; (2) problems when no candidate has a majority of electors, including that each state would cast only one vote in the

House of Representatives, that the vice president is selected by a different method, and that DC would not participate in the contingent election; and (3) that there is no provision for a candidate dying just before or after the November election.

President Johnson concluded, "Elimination of these defects in our Constitution are [sic] long overdue. Our concepts of self-government and sound government require it."[45]

In recognition of these concerns, the American Bar Association undertook a study on the subject and published a report recommending elimination of the Electoral College in January 1967. That month, Gallup asked people whether they would "approve or disapprove of an amendment to the Constitution which would do away with the Electoral College and base the election of a president on the total popular vote cast throughout the nation." Fifty-eight percent approved and 22 percent disapproved of such an amendment. Gallup asked the identical question five more times, and in each iteration, a solid majority approved of the amendment to eliminate the Electoral College. (See Table 2.)

Louis Harris asked three questions in November 1968 that appear to have been asked before the election. In one, Harris explained, "If the Electoral College can't elect a president, the House of Representatives names the President with each state, no matter how big or small, having one vote." Sixty percent said they opposed this system, while 24 percent favored it.

In another question, Harris told people: "It has been suggested that the election system be changed so that whoever receives the most votes would be President, provided he gets 40 percent or more of the vote. Otherwise there would be a run-off election between the two highest candidates." Sixty-three percent said they favored changing the system, and 21 percent were opposed.

The third question: "Suppose no candidate receives a majority of the Electoral College vote for president this time. Would you favor the man who received the most popular votes being named President or would you rather see the three candidates negotiate with each other in the Electoral College?" Seventy-two percent wanted to elect the man with the most votes, while 14 percent preferred negotiating with the Electoral College.

The questions from this period usually coincided with interest from the president or Congress in changing the system by which we elect the

Table 2. Gallup Polls on the Electoral College, 1967–80

Q: *Would you approve or disapprove of an amendment to the Constitution which would do away with the Electoral College and base the election of a president on the total popular vote cast throughout the nation?*

	Approve of a Constitutional Amendment	Disapprove of a Constitutional Amendment	No Opinion
January 1967	58%	22%	20%
October 1967	65	22	13
May 1968	66	19	15
November 1968*	80	12	8
January 1977	73	15	12
November 1980*	67	19	15

Note: The November 1968 and November 1980 questions were asked after the presidential elections in those years.
Source: Gallup Organization, latest that of November 1980.

president. Sen. Birch Bayh (D-IN), who championed eliminating the Electoral College through much of his career, introduced legislation in 1969 and again in 1977 and 1979 to do so. In addition to Gallup's questions, Harris asked a question about it in late April and early May 1977. Harris' question referred to the changes the newly elected President Jimmy Carter had asked be made in federal election law, including eliminating the Electoral College. In the poll, 74 percent favored "passing a constitutional amendment to abolish the Electoral College and have the President and Vice President elected by popular vote," while 13 percent were opposed. It was more popular than the other options Harris asked about, including publicly financing all primary and general elections for the House and Senate (49 percent favored this and 28 percent were opposed), loosening the law on public financing of presidential elections to allow candidates to raise more money locally (40 and 33 percent, respectively), and eliminating the Hatch Act prohibition on political activity by permanent federal employees (34 to 27 percent).

A December 1980 survey from Harris asked about proposed changes in our system of elections. Seventy-seven percent favored "having a president chosen by popular vote, instead of determining the outcome by electoral votes for each state," while 21 percent were opposed.

A handful of questions were asked about the Electoral College in the 1990s when President George H. W. Bush faced Bill Clinton and H. Ross Perot. Several were asked in the summer of 1992. In July, CBS News and *New York Times* interviewers asked people what should happen if none of the candidates running in 1992 got an Electoral College majority and Congress had to vote for president. Twenty-nine percent said the representative from their district should vote for the candidate who got the most votes nationwide, 16 percent for the one who carried their state, 14 percent for the one who carried their district, and a third for the candidate who would make the best president.

In another question from *Time*/CNN/Yankelovich in June 1992, registered voters were told that "if Perot runs, there is a chance that no presidential candidate will get enough electoral votes to win. If that happens, the Constitution gives the House of Representatives the power to decide who will be the next president." Thirty-one percent of registered voters said this was fair, while 61 percent said the Constitution should be changed. NBC News/*Wall Street Journal* pollsters also asked people in July how their representatives should vote. A third of registered voters said for the candidate who received the most votes in their district, 32 percent for the national winner, and 22 percent according to their own conscience. In Gallup's question from June 1992, also asked of registered voters, 12 percent said for the candidate who won their district, 52 percent for the candidate who won the most votes nationally, and 13 percent for the candidate who won their state and separately for the candidate nominated by the representative's political party.

Princeton Survey Research Associates for *Newsweek* in 1995 asked people about the goals of a new party that Ross Perot wanted to create. Just 13 percent of the registered voters surveyed said getting rid of the Electoral College should be the new party's most important goal, while another 38 percent said it should be one of several important goals. A plurality, 44 percent, said this was not an important goal.

The 2000 Election

Days before the 2000 election, in which George W. Bush faced Al Gore, Princeton Survey Research Associates/*Newsweek* pollsters told registered voters it was possible for a presidential candidate to finish second in the national popular vote but still capture electoral votes in enough states to win the White House. They were asked, if Al Gore or George W. Bush were to be elected president in this way, whether it would seriously hurt his ability to be an effective national leader. Twenty-one percent said it would, but 69 percent said it would not.

In a November 3–5 poll, 57 percent favored the candidate who won the popular vote serving as the next president; 33 percent favored the candidate who won the electoral vote. In this NBC News/*Wall Street Journal* question, people were told: "As you may know, presidents are chosen not by direct popular vote, but by the Electoral College system in which each state receives electoral votes based on its population. Over the past one hundred years, the winning presidential candidate has won both the popular and electoral vote."

After the disputed George W. Bush–Al Gore presidential election, a few pollsters explored public views about the Electoral College, but their focus was mostly on other aspects of the 2000 imbroglio.

With the passage of nearly 20 years' time since that election, it is worth briefly reviewing how the public reacted. This helps put the questions asked about the Electoral College into context. On five separate occasions, Gallup/CNN/*USA Today* pollsters asked whether the situation that occurred because of the election was "a constitutional crisis, a major problem for the country but not a constitutional crisis, a minor problem, or not a problem at all." No more than 17 percent ever described the situation as a constitutional crisis; most people saw it as a major or minor problem.

Between November 11 and December 13 when the Supreme Court acted and Al Gore conceded, in four polls conducted by the same pollster, large majorities said they would accept George W. Bush, and separately, Al Gore, as the legitimate president if either man were declared the winner. In nine questions asked by CBS News and the *New York Times* between December 2000 and January 2004, majorities ranging from 51 to 57 percent said George W. Bush legitimately won the election. In the questions that were asked, the public supported amending the Constitution to elect the president directly. (See Table 3.)

In mid-November 2000 after the election, for example, 61 percent of those surveyed told Gallup in thinking about the way in which the president is elected, they preferred "to amend the Constitution so the candidate who receives the most total votes nationwide wins the election," while 35 percent preferred "to keep the current system in which the candidate who wins the most votes in the Electoral College wins the election." Republicans were less likely to approve of its elimination (44 percent) than independents (62 percent) or Democrats (73 percent). A majority of all ideological groups favored an amendment, with conservatives less enthusiastic (53 percent) than moderates (64 percent) and liberals (67 percent). Age differences were modest. Those with a college education or more were less enthusiastic about amending the Constitution for this purpose than those with some college or a high school education or less.

A few other post-2000 election polls with different question wording also revealed more support than opposition for amending the Constitution, as Table 3 shows.

In 2004, in anticipation of that election, ABC News and NBC News/*Wall Street Journal* pollsters asked people about their preferences. In both polls, around half thought the president should be elected by the popular vote and around four in 10 through the Electoral College. In two 2012 surveys, the popular vote was also more popular than the Electoral College.

The 2016 Election

Since 2000, Gallup has asked its question about the Electoral College four more times (Table 4). In each case, more people favored amending the Constitution so that the candidate who receives the most total votes nationwide wins the election.

What is noteworthy here is the depth of partisan divisions in the organization's 2016 and 2019 questions. In Gallup's poll conducted in late November 2016 after the contentious Donald Trump versus Hillary Clinton contest, people were evenly divided, with 49 percent favoring an amendment and 47 percent the status quo. The electorate was deeply divided by

Table 3. The Electoral College and the 2000 Election

Q: *As you may know, presidents are chosen not by direct popular vote, but by the Electoral College system, in which each state receives electoral votes based on its population. In this election, Al Gore won the popular vote, and George W. Bush appears to have won the electoral vote. Would you favor passing a Constitutional amendment that would determine the winner of the (2000) presidential election by popular vote, or would you rather continue the current system, which determines the winner by electoral votes?* (NBC News/Wall Street Journal)

Q: *Thinking for a moment about the way in which the president is elected in this country, which would you prefer—to amend the Constitution so the candidate who receives the most total votes nationwide wins the election, or to keep the current system, in which the candidate who wins the most votes in the Electoral College wins the election?* (Gallup/CNN/USA Today)

Q: *Presidents are elected by the Electoral College, in which each state gets as many votes as it has members of Congress and can cast all of them for whoever wins in that state. Do you think we should keep the Electoral College, or should we amend the Constitution and elect as President whoever gets the most votes in the whole country?* (CBS/New York Times)

		Amend the Constitution	Keep the Current System
NBC News/*Wall Street Journal*	November 3–5	57%	33%
	December 7–10	50	44
Gallup/CNN/*USA Today*	November 11–12	61	35
	December 15–17	59	37
CBS News/*New York Times*	November 10–12	60	31
	November 27–28	57	35
	December 9–10*	57	39

Note: All questions were asked of national adults. *The December question was asked by CBS News only.
Source: NBC News/*Wall Street Journal*, November and December 2000; Gallup/CNN/*USA Today*, November and December 2000; and CBS News/*New York Times*, November and December 2000.

Table 4. Gallup Polls on the Electoral College Since 2000

Q: *Thinking for a moment about the way in which the president is elected in this country, which would you prefer—to amend the Constitution so the candidate who receives the most total votes nationwide wins the election, [or] to keep the current system, in which the candidate who wins the most votes in the Electoral College wins the election?*

	Amend the Constitution			Keep the Current System
	Total	Democrats	Republicans	D-R Gap	Total
November 2000	61%	73%	44%	29%	35%
December 2000	59	75	41	34	37
2004	61	73	46	27	35
2011	62	71	53	18	35
2016	49	81	19	62	47
2019	55	84	24	60	43

Note: All samples are national adults. The November and December 2000 questions were asked after the election, with the November survey occurring November 11–12, 2000, and the December survey on December 15–17, 2000.
Source: Gallup Organization, latest that of April 2019.

party that year, with 81 percent of Democrats favoring the amendment, compared to only 19 percent of Republicans, for a 62 percentage-point gap. In their 2019 question, the gap was 60 points. After the 2000 election was decided, the partisan gap was much smaller. The gap was also much smaller in previous iterations of the question.

Other pollsters asked about the Electoral College in the aftermath of the 2016 election. The results are presented in Table 5.

The Current Debate

In the spring of 2019, two pollsters explored opinions about the National Popular Vote Interstate Compact, an agreement of a number of states and the District of Columbia to award the electoral votes of their state to the candidate who wins the national popular vote. The compact is the brainchild

Table 5. Other Questions on the Electoral College Taken in or After 2016

Q: *Thinking for a moment about the way in which the president is elected in this country, which would you prefer—to amend the constitution so the candidate who receives the most total votes nationwide wins the election, or to keep the current system, in which the candidate who wins the most votes in the Electoral College wins the election?* (CNN/ORC)

Q: *For future presidential elections, would you support or oppose changing to a system in which the president is elected by direct popular vote, instead of by the Electoral College?* (Quinnipiac University)

Q: *Do you think the Electoral College, which ultimately decides who will be president, is still the best way to elect the leader, or do you think the president should be decided by the popular vote?* (Bloomberg)

Q: *Thinking about future elections, do you think who wins the presidency should be determined by: The electoral college, where the electors or representatives from each state vote for the candidate who won the most votes in the state, or the popular vote, that is, the candidate who gets the most votes in the nation regardless of the state in which people live.* (Marist/McClatchy)

Q: *Do you believe the United States should change the Constitution so the president is elected by the popular vote, not through the Electoral College?* (Suffolk/ USA Today)

Q: *For future elections, do you favor or oppose abolishing the Electoral College and instead electing the president based on the popular vote?* (Fox News)

Q: *Presidents are elected by the Electoral College, in which each state gets as many votes as it has members of Congress and can cast all of them for whoever wins in that state. Do you think we should keep the Electoral College, or should we amend the Constitution and elect as President whoever gets the most votes in the whole country?* (CBS News)

(*Continued on next page*)

(Continued from previous page)

Table 5. Other Questions on the Electoral College Taken in or After 2016

Q: Do you believe presidential elections should be decided based on the popular vote or by the Electoral College? (Associated Press/NORC)

	Amend the Constitution/ Support a Popular Vote	Keep the Current System
November 2016		
CNN/ORC	51%	44%
Quinnipiac	53	39
December 2016		
Bloomberg	54%	41%
Marist/McClatchy	52	45
Suffolk/*USA Today*	42	50
Fox News	46	45
AP/NORC	69	30
CBS News	54	41

Note: The CNN/ORC, Bloomberg, AP/NORC, and CBS News questions were asked of national adults. The Quinnipiac University, Marist, Suffolk University, and Fox News questions were asked of registered voters.
Source: CNN/ORC, November 2016; Quinnipiac, November 2016; Bloomberg, December 2016; Marist/McClatchy, December 2016; Suffolk University/*USA Today*, December 2016; Fox News, December 2016; CBS News, December 2016; and AP/NORC, December 2016.

of John Koza, who formed National Popular Vote, a nonprofit 501(c)(4) to promote the idea.[46] This approach obviates the difficult process of amending the Constitution. Article II of the Constitution gives states the authority to determine how their electoral votes are awarded, so the states that have passed legislation to agree to the National Popular Vote Interstate Compact would award their to electors' votes to the winner of the national popular vote.

As of July 2019, 16 jurisdictions with 196 electoral votes (270 are necessary to win) have joined the compact. Eight states have tried to pass legislation to effect the change and failed. In 2020, in Colorado, a citizen-generated ballot measure will decide whether the state should stay in the National Popular Vote Interstate Compact. If it passes, it would overturn a law passed in 2019.

In March 2019, Morning Consult and *Politico* asked people first whether presidential elections should be based on the Electoral College or the national popular vote and then about the compact. Fifty percent in the online poll said they should be based on the national popular vote and 34 percent the Electoral College. In the other question, the pollsters mentioned the compact by name. (See Table 6.) In this question, 43 percent said the US should embrace the compact, and 33 percent wanted to keep the Electoral College. Democrats were more enthusiastic than Republicans about the compact.

Gallup split its sample and asked one-half about amending the Constitution and the other about the National Popular Vote Interstate Compact proposal. Fifty-five percent, in line with Gallup's previous questions, favored amending the Constitution, while 43 percent wanted to keep the current system. Gallup did not mention the National Popular Vote Interstate Compact by name, but in describing it, 45 percent were in favor, and 53 percent were opposed. According to Gallup, the gap in support for the two approaches "stems from Democrats being less supportive of the compact approach than the amendment route. Republicans show similar levels of opposition to basing the winner on the popular vote with both proposals."

In both polls, the compact idea was more popular than keeping the Electoral College. There were substantial differences between the two surveys in terms of responses. This could be explained by different question wording, by online versus traditional polling method, or by the fact that Gallup split its sample. But it is also possible that people have not given much thought to the compact and that poll responses will bounce around.

In July 2019, Claster Consulting released a poll of voters who said they will definitely or probably vote in the 2020 election. The poll, commissioned by the National Popular Vote Interstate Compact, found that 71 percent nationally, including 81 percent of Democrats, 67 percent of independents, and 61 percent of Republicans, said that "the person who gets the most votes nationwide should become president." Thirty-two percent of Republicans, 23 percent of independents, and 10 percent of Democrats disagreed.

Table 6. Amending the Constitution or the National Popular Vote Interstate Compact

Q: *As you may know, the winner of the presidential election is determined by the Electoral College, in which states are allocated electoral votes based on their number of senators and representatives in Congress. These votes are cast by electors or representative for the winner of the popular vote in the state, where the candidate with the highest number of electoral votes wins the election. Knowing this, do you believe presidential elections should be based on the Electoral College or the national popular vote?* (Morning Consult/Politico)

Q: *As you may know, a dozen states have signed onto the National Popular Vote Interstate Compact, an agreement that requires states to award their Electoral College votes to whomever wins the most votes nationwide. Knowing this, do you think the United States should keep the Electoral College and the current way we elect presidents, or have states award their Electoral College votes to whomever wins the most votes nationwide?* (Morning Consult/Politico)

Q: *Thinking for a moment about the way in which the president is elected in this country, which would you prefer—to amend the Constitution so the candidate who receives the most total votes nationwide wins the election, [or] to keep the current system, in which the candidate who wins the most votes in the Electoral College wins the election?* (Gallup)

Q: *Next, as you may know, some states are considering changing the way they award electoral votes in presidential elections. Under the proposal, the Electoral College would remain, but the states would award their electoral votes to the winner of the popular vote nationwide rather than awarding them to the candidate who received the most votes in their state. Would you be for or against this change?* (Gallup)

	—————— Responses of ——————			
	Total	Republicans	Democrats	Independents
Morning Consult/ Politico	—	—	—	—
National popular vote	50%	30%	72%	46%

(Continued on next page)

(Continued from previous page)

Table 6. Amending the Constitution or the National Popular Vote Interstate Compact

	Total	Republicans	Democrats	Independents
			Responses of	
Keep the Electoral College	34	57	16	29
States award votes to national popular vote winner	43	23	65	40
Keep the Electoral College	33	57	14	31
Gallup	—	—	—	—
Prefer the popular vote amendment	55	25	84	57
Prefer to keep the current system	43	75	13	41
For the state proposal	45	20	69	45
Against the state proposal	53	79	30	52

Note: Morning Consult/*Politico* questions were asked of registered voters, and Gallup questions were asked of national adults. In the Gallup responses, "Republicans" include Republican leaners, and "Democrats" include Democratic leaners.
Source: Morning Consult/*Politico*, March 2019; and Gallup Organization, April 2019.

In another question, respondents were told:

Fifteen states and Washington, DC have passed the National Popular Vote Compact, which would ensure that the winner of the national popular vote becomes president. Do you support or oppose using the national popular vote to decide who the president should be?

Likely voters were less enthusiastic. Sixty-two percent said they supported the idea, while 26 percent were opposed. The pollster also

Table 7. The National Popular Vote Initiative

Q: *Do you think the person who gets the most votes nationwide should become president?*

Q: *Fifteen states and Washington, DC have passed the National Popular Vote Interstate Compact, which would ensure that the winner of the national popular vote becomes president. Do you support or oppose using the national popular vote to decide who the president should be?*

		Responses of		
	Total	Republicans	Democrats	Independents
Person who gets the most votes should become president	71%	61%	83%	67%
Disagree	21	32	10	23
National Popular Vote Interstate Compact				
Support using national popular vote to decide who the president should be	62%	49%	79%	55%
Oppose	26	41	10	29

Note: Sample is likely voters.
Source: Claster Consulting for the National Popular Vote Interstate Compact, July 2019.

tested 15 pro–National Public Vote arguments and eight anti–National Public Vote messages.

According to the Roper Center at Cornell polling data archive, two other pollsters explored continuing to use the Electoral College or amending the Constitution to determine the winner by national popular vote. In the NBC News/*Wall Street Journal*'s late April–early May poll, 53 percent favored an amendment, while 43 percent favored continuing to use the Electoral College. In a July NPR/PBS *NewsHour*/Marist poll, 42 percent said "getting rid of the electoral college as part of the presidential election process" was a good idea, and 50 percent said it was a bad idea. In their December question, the responses were 44 and 48 percent, respectively.

How Pressing of an Issue?

Although there has been consistent support in polls for amending the Constitution to directly elect the president, election reform in general and eliminating the Electoral College specifically do not seem to energize many voters. In Gallup's monthly open-ended question about the most important problem facing the country in 2019, for example, no more than 1 percent of respondents have ever mentioned election reform or election-related issues.

In a question asked by NBC News and the *Wall Street Journal* in June 2019, 56 percent said electing the president directly would make democracy work better, but other reforms were more popular. Replacing the Electoral College with a nationwide popular vote ranked as the sixth most popular option out of eight proposals in the poll for improving democracy and had the highest percentage of opposition; 27 percent said it would make democracy worse. More popular options for improving democracy were having term limits for members of Congress (71 percent said this would improve democracy) and separately for Supreme Court justices (60 percent), having nonpartisan commissions draw congressional district lines (66 percent), making Election Day a national holiday (66 percent), and enacting automatic voter registration (65 percent).

In Gallup's April 2019 question, the pollsters asked how concerned Americans are with four different aspects of the Electoral College. The highest level of deep concern (37 percent said they were "very" concerned) was that the winner of the popular vote does not always win the election. Twenty-six percent were somewhat concerned, 15 percent not too concerned, and 22 percent not concerned at all (Table 8).

Conclusion

American public opinion has been remarkably consistent on the Electoral College in the questions that have been asked. The public prefers direct election of the president to the Electoral College mechanism.

That said, there are significant gaps in public understanding. We do not know from recent polls, for example, how knowledgeable Americans are

Table 8. Concerns About the Electoral College System

Q: *How concerned are you about each of the following aspects of the US Electoral College system—very concerned, somewhat concerned, not too concerned, or not concerned at all?*

	Very Concerned	Somewhat Concerned	Not Too Concerned	Not Concerned at All
The winner of the popular vote doesn't always win the election	37%	26%	15%	22%
Small-population states have a disproportionate influence on the outcome	35	29	20	16
It makes it very difficult for independent or third-party candidates to win	32	29	20	19
Candidates mostly focus their campaigns on voters in a small number of competitive "swing" states	27	30	26	17

Note: Sample is likely voters.
Source: Claster Consulting for the National Popular Vote Interstate Compact, July 2019.

about the Electoral College. Nor do we have many polls that balance arguments for or against the Electoral College.

Additionally, in 2000, Americans believed the winner under the Electoral College system was the legitimate president, and in a few other questions, people do not appear to believe that a president's effectiveness would be compromised by an Electoral College win. That notwithstanding, Americans like the idea of directly electing their president.

About the Authors

John C. Fortier is the director of governmental studies at the Bipartisan Policy Center, where he directed the Commission on Political Reform. He was previously a research fellow at the American Enterprise Institute (AEI), where he also served as executive director of the Continuity of Government Commission, principal contributor to the AEI-Brookings Election Reform Project, and participant in AEI's Election Watch. He was the director of the Center for the Study of American Democracy at Kenyon College and taught at the University of Pennsylvania, University of Delaware, Harvard University, and Boston College. Fortier served as an adviser to the President's Commission on Election Administration and a member of the American Law Institute's Project on Election Administration. He is the editor of the third edition of *After the People Vote: A Guide to the Electoral College* (AEI Press, 2004) and author of *Absentee and Early Voting: Trends, Promises, and Perils* (AEI Press, 2006), as well as other books and scholarly and popular articles. He is a frequent radio and television commentator on Congress, the presidency, and elections.

Walter Berns was a resident scholar at the American Enterprise Institute. He taught at Georgetown University, University of Toronto, Cornell University, and Yale University. His government service included membership on the National Council on the Humanities, the Council of Scholars in the Library of Congress, and the Judicial Fellows Commission. In 1983, he was a US delegate to the United Nations Commission on Human Rights. He was a Guggenheim, Rockefeller, and Fulbright fellow and a Phi Beta Kappa lecturer. He authored numerous articles on American government in both professional and popular journals; his books include *Making Patriots* (University of Chicago Press, 2001), *Taking the Constitution Seriously*

(Simon & Schuster, 1987), and *In Defense of Liberal Democracy* (AEI Press, 1984). He was the editor of the first and second editions of *After the People Vote: A Guide to the Electoral College*. Berns passed away in 2015.

Akhil Reed Amar is Sterling Professor of Law and Political Science at Yale University, where he teaches constitutional law in both Yale College and Yale Law School. He is a member of the American Academy of Arts and Sciences and a recipient of the American Bar Foundation's Outstanding Scholar Award. He is the author of dozens of law review articles and several books, including *The Constitution Today: Timeless Lessons for the Issues of Our Era* (Basic Books, 2016), named one of the year's top 10 nonfiction books by *Time* magazine; *The Law of the Land: A Grand Tour of Our Constitutional Republic* (Basic Books, 2015); *America's Unwritten Constitution: The Precedents and Principles We Live by* (Basic Books, 2012), named one of the year's 100 best nonfiction books by the *Washington Post*; *America's Constitution: A Biography* (Random House, 2005), winner of the American Bar Association's Silver Gavel Award; *The Bill of Rights: Creation and Reconstruction* (Yale University Press, 1998), winner of the Yale University Press Governors' Award; and *The Constitution and Criminal Procedure: First Principles* (Yale University Press, 1997).

Vikram David Amar joined the University of Illinois College of Law as its dean in 2015, after having been a professor of law for many years at law schools in the University of California system, most recently the University of California, Davis, School of Law, where he served as senior associate dean for academic affairs. He has produced several books and over 60 articles in leading law reviews. He is a coauthor (with Akhil Reed Amar and Steven Calabresi) of the upcoming sixth edition of the six-volume *Treatise on Constitutional Law* (West Publishing Co., 2021), pioneered by Ron Rotunda and John Nowak, as well as the hardbound and soft-cover one-volume hornbooks that derive from it. He is also a coauthor (with Jonathan Varat) of *Constitutional Law: Cases and Materials* (Foundation Press, 2017), a coauthor on multiple volumes of the Wright & Miller *Federal Practice and Procedure Treatise* (West Publishing Co., 2006), and a coauthor (with John Oakley) of *American Civil Procedure* (Kluwer Law International, 2008).

Karlyn Bowman is a resident fellow at the American Enterprise Institute. She compiles and analyzes American public opinion using available polling data on a variety of subjects, including the economy, taxes, the state of workers in America, the environment and global warming, attitudes about homosexuality and gay marriage, NAFTA and free trade, the war in Iraq, and women's attitudes. In addition, Bowman has studied and spoken about the evolution of American politics because of key demographic and geographic changes. She was managing editor of *Public Opinion* and editor of the *American Enterprise*. She has often lectured on the role of think tanks in the United States and writes a weekly column for Forbes.com.

Martin Diamond died in 1977 just before he was to assume the Leavey Chair on the Foundations of American Freedom at Georgetown University. He taught at the University of Chicago, Illinois Institute of Technology, Claremont Men's College, Claremont Graduate School, and Northern Illinois University. Diamond also served as a fellow for the Center for Advanced Study in the Behavioral Sciences, the Rockefeller Foundation, the Realm Foundation, the Woodrow Wilson International Center for Scholars, and the National Humanities Institute. A frequent adviser to private and public agencies and to local, state, and federal officials, including senators, congressmen, and presidents and vice presidents of the United States, he spent the last morning of his life testifying before a Senate committee on the Electoral College. His essays appear in *As Far as Republican Principles Will Admit: Essays by Martin Diamond* (AEI Press, 1992).

Norman J. Ornstein is a resident scholar at the American Enterprise Institute (AEI), where he studies politics, elections, and the US Congress. He is a cohost of AEI's Election Watch series, a contributing editor and columnist for National Journal and the *Atlantic*, a BBC News election analyst, and the chairman of the Campaign Legal Center. Ornstein previously served as codirector of the AEI-Brookings Election Reform Project and senior counselor to the Continuity of Government Commission. His articles and opinion pieces have been published widely, including in *Politico*, the *New York Times*, *New York Daily News*, the *Wall Street Journal*, and the *Washington Post*. His books include the bestsellers *One Nation After Trump: A Guide for the Perplexed, the Disillusioned, the Desperate, and the Not-Yet*

Deported, with E. J. Dionne and Thomas E. Mann (St. Martin's Press, 2017); *It's Even Worse Than It Looks: How the American Constitutional System Collided with the New Politics of Extremism* (Basic Books, 2012); *The Broken Branch: How Congress Is Failing America and How to Get It Back on Track*, with Thomas E. Mann (Oxford University Press, 2006); and *The Permanent Campaign and Its Future* (AEI Press, 2000).

Notes

1. In Maine, each of the two congressional districts chooses one elector, and two are elected at large. This means that the state's four electoral votes will be cast for one candidate or three will be cast for one candidate and one for another candidate. In Nebraska, each of the three congressional districts chooses an elector, and two are elected at large.

2. The case, *McPherson v. Blacker*, 146 US 1 (1892), dealt with the various methods of choosing electors that the states so far had adopted. On state authority respecting the methods of choosing presidential electors, see also *Burroughs v. United States*, 290 US 534, 544 (1934). On congressional authority to regulate voting in presidential elections—if electors are chosen by popular vote—see, for example, *Oregon v. Mitchell*, 400 US 112 (1970); and *Williams v. Rhodes*, 393 US 23 (1968). Only Justice William O. Douglas has cast doubt on the unrestricted authority of the states to determine how electors shall be chosen. Speaking for himself alone in *Williams v. Rhodes*, he said: "It is necessary in this case to decide . . . whether states may select [electors] through appointment rather than by popular vote, or whether there is a constitutional right to vote for them."

3. In Wichita Falls, Texas, between Grant and Garfield Streets and running parallel with them, there is both a Tilden Street *and* a Hayes Street, which suggests either a fine sense of historical propriety, a sharply and equally divided city council at the time this section of the city was being planned, or a doubt as to how the electoral commission would decide.

4. *Bush v. Gore* emphasized the parties' agreement to the case that the Florida state legislature intended to have its recounts completed by six days before the electors cast their votes to meet this "safe harbor."

5. See Fair Vote, "Faithless Elector State Laws," https://www.fairvote.org/faithless_elector_state_laws.

6. See William Josephson and Beverly Ross, "Repairing the Electoral College," *Journal of Legislation* 22 (1996): 145.

7. Sanford Levinson and Ernest Young, "Who's Afraid of the Twelfth Amendment?," *Florida State University Law Review* 29 (Fall 2001): 935. See *Jones v. Bush*, 122 F. Supp. 2d 713 (N.D. Tex. 2000). Summarily affirmed by Fifth Circuit, *Jones v. Bush*, 244 F.3d 134 (5th Cir. 2000).

8. Levinson and Young, "Who's Afraid of the Twelfth Amendment?," 938.

9. The president of the Senate is, of course, the vice president of the United States, and it sometimes happens that he is required to supervise the counting of electoral votes and announce the results of an election in which he was himself a candidate. In recent years, Richard Nixon (January 6, 1961) and Al Gore (January 6, 2001) announced their defeats for the presidency, and Walter Mondale (January 6, 1981) and Dan Quayle (January 6, 1993) announced their defeats for the vice presidency. George H. W. Bush (January 5, 1989) was in the happy position of announcing himself to be president-elect; he was the first president of the Senate to do so since Martin Van Buren in 1837.

10. Abraham Lincoln, *Complete Works of Abraham Lincoln*, ed. John G. Nicolay and John Hay (New York: Lamb Publishing Co., 1905), 11:8–9.

11. Presidents must be natural-born citizens of at least 35 years of age and have lived in the United States for at least 14 years.

12. *Colorado Department of State v. Baca*, No. 19-518 (2020); and *Chiafolo v. Washington*, No. 19-465 (2020).

13. See Akhil Amar, "Presidents, Vice Presidents, and Death: Closing the Constitution's Succession Gap," *Arkansas Law Review* 48 (1995): 215.

14. See, for example, John R. Koza et al., *Every Vote Equal: A State-Based Plan for Electing the President by National Popular Vote* (Los Altos, CA: National Popular Vote Press, 2011).

15. See, for example, Norman R. Williams, "Why the National Popular Vote Compact Is Unconstitutional," *Brigham Young University Law Review* 2012, no. 5 (2012), https://digitalcommons.law.byu.edu/cgi/viewcontent.cgi?article=2686&context=lawreview.

16. National Population Vote, "Status of National Popular Vote Bill in Each State," https://www.nationalpopularvote.com/state-status.

17. Portions of this account of the election of 1824 are adapted from an article in *Fortune* magazine in 1980 by Norman Ornstein and Richard Brody.

18. Since each elector casts two votes, two candidates could receive the vote of a majority of electors.

19. Harold C. Syrett et al., eds., *The Papers of Alexander Hamilton* (New York and London: Columbia University Press, 1961), 25:275.

20. Henry Clay, letter in the *National Intelligencer*, January 31, 1825.

21. Andrew Jackson, letter to William B. Lewis, February 14, 1825.

22. See William H. Rehnquist, *Centennial Crisis: The Disputed Election of 1876* (New York: Alfred A. Knopf, 2004), 97.

23. The materials that describe the chronology of events in this chapter can be found in many public sources and news accounts. Especially helpful was the account in Political Staff of the *Washington Post*, *Deadlock: The Inside Story of America's Closest Election* (Washington, DC: Public Affairs, 2001). This book relied heavily on the reporting of the *Washington Post*'s team. Also helpful was E. J. Dionne Jr. and William Kristol, eds., *Bush v. Gore: The Court Cases and Commentary* (Washington, DC: Brookings Institution Press, 2001).

24. *Bush v. Gore*, 531 US 98 (2000).

25. *Bush v. Gore*, 531 US 98 (2000).

26. Walter Berns, "Let's Hear It for the Electoral College," *Wall Street Journal*, December 2, 1992, https://www.aei.org/articles/lets-hear-it-for-the-electoral-college/.

27. An earlier version of this chapter was published in Gary L. Gregg, ed., *Securing Democracy: Why We Have an Electoral College* (Wilmington, DE: ISI Books, 2001).

28. Henry F. Graff, *Grover Cleveland* (New York: Times Books, 2002), 95.

29. This chapter was adapted from two articles published at FindLaw.com on November 30 and December 14, 2001. Akhil Reed Amar and Vikram David Amar, "History, Slavery, Sexism, the South, and the Electoral College: Part One of a Three-Part Series on the 2000 Election and the Electoral College," FindLaw.com, November 30, 2001; and Akhil Reed Amar and Vikram David Amar, "A Critique of the Top Ten

Modern Arguments for the Electoral College: Part Two of a Three-Part Series on the 2000 Election and the Electoral College," FindLaw.com, December 14, 2001.

30. Max Farrand, ed., *The Records of the Federal Convention of 1787* (New Haven, CT: Yale University Press, 1966), 1:486.

31. Farrand, ed., *The Records of the Federal Convention of 1787*, 1:68–69.

32. Farrand, ed., *The Records of the Federal Convention of 1787*, 1:56–57.

33. *Annals of Congress*, 8th Cong., 1st sess., 537–38.

34. Akhil Reed Amar and Vikram David Amar, "How to Achieve Direct National Election of the President Without Amending the Constitution: Part Three of a Three-Part Series on the 2000 Election and the Electoral College," FindLaw, December 28, 2001, https://supreme.findlaw.com/legal-commentary/how-to-achieve-direct-national-election-of-the-president-without-amending-the-constitution.html.

35. *The Electoral College and the American Idea of Democracy* was originally published as a booklet by the American Enterprise Institute in 1977.

36. See Max Farrand, ed., *The Records of the Federal Convention of 1787* (New Haven, CT: Yale University Press, 1966), 1:68–69, 80; 2:29–31, 56–57, 111.

37. The "confederalists" won a temporary and partial victory at the convention when the express provision for popular election of the electors was barely defeated. Farrand, ed., *The Records of the Federal Convention of 1787*, 2:404. The Constitution finally provided that electors be elected "in such manner" as the state legislatures might decide. During the first three elections, electors were typically chosen by the state legislatures. By 1824, in all but six of the then 24 states, electors were being popularly elected. Ever since 1832, popular election has been the universal rule, with negligible exceptions.

38. For example, see James Wilson's explanation of the electoral device to the Pennsylvania ratifying convention. Farrand, ed., *The Records of the Federal Convention of 1787*, 3:167.

39. See the remarks of Madison and Oliver Ellsworth. Farrand, ed., *The Records of the Federal Convention of 1787*, 2:111.

40. Farrand, ed., *The Records of the Federal Convention of 1787*, 2:57.

41. Alexander Bickel wisely stressed the importance of the Electoral College to federalism in *Reform and Continuity: The Electoral College, the Convention, and the Party System* (New York: Harper Colophon Books, 1971). See also the excellent discussions in Judith Best, *The Case Against the Direct Election of the President: A Defense of the Electoral College* (Ithaca: Cornell University Press, 1975), 199ff. and 133ff.; and Wallace S. Sayre and Judith H. Parris, *Voting for President: The Electoral College in the American Political System* (Washington, DC: Brookings Institution, 1970), 51ff.

42. American Bar Association, "Electing the President: Recommendations of the American Bar Association's Commission on Electoral College Reform," *American Bar Association Journal* 53, no. 3 (March 1967), 37, https://www.jstor.org/stable/25723942?seq=1. The essay from which these excerpts are taken was written in response to this American Bar Association report.

43. The data used in this chapter come from the poll database of the Roper Center at Cornell University and from the author's files.

44. Lyndon B. Johnson, "Special Message to the Congress Proposing Constitutional Amendments Relating to Terms for House Members and the Electoral

College System" (speech, Washington, DC, January 20, 1966), University of California, Santa Barbara, American Presidency Project, https://www.presidency.ucsb.edu/documents/special-message-the-congress-proposing-constitutional-amendments-relating-terms-for-house.

45. Johnson, "Special Message to the Congress Proposing Constitutional Amendments Relating to Terms for House Members and the Electoral College System."

46. National Popular Vote, "Agreement Among the States to Elect the President by National Popular Vote," https://www.nationalpopularvote.com/written-explanation.

Appendix A

Provisions in the Constitution for Presidential Selection

Article II

Section 1. The executive power shall be vested in a President of the United States of America. He shall hold his office during the term of four years, and, together with the Vice President, chosen for the same term, be elected, as follows:

Each state shall appoint, in such manner as the Legislature thereof may direct, a number of electors, equal to the whole number of Senators and Representatives to which the State may be entitled in the Congress: but no Senator or Representative, or person holding an office of trust or profit under the United States, shall be appointed an elector.

The 12th Amendment
(Ratified June 15, 1804)

The Electors shall meet in their respective states, and vote by ballot for President and Vice-President, one of whom, at least, shall not be an inhabitant of the same state with themselves; they shall name in their ballots the person voted for as President and in distinct ballots the person voted for as Vice-President, and they shall make distinct lists of all persons voted for as President, and of all persons voted for as Vice-President, and of the number of votes for each, which lists they shall sign and certify, and transmit sealed to the seat of the government of the United States, directed to the President of the Senate;—The President of the Senate shall, in the presence of the Senate and House of Representatives, open all the certificates and the votes shall then be counted;—The person having the greatest number of votes for President, shall be the President, if such number be a majority of the whole number of Electors appointed; and if no person have such majority, then from the persons having the highest numbers not exceeding three on the list of those voted for as President, the House of Representatives shall choose immediately, by ballot, the President. But in choosing the President, the votes shall be taken by states, the representation from each state having one vote; a quorum for this purpose shall consist of a member or members from two-thirds of the states, and a majority of all the states shall be necessary to a choice. And if the House of Representatives shall not choose a President whenever the right of choice shall devolve upon them, before the fourth day of March next following, then the Vice-President shall act as President, as in the case of the death or other constitutional disability of the President.—The person having the greatest number of votes as Vice-President, shall be the Vice-President, if such number be a majority of the whole number of Electors appointed, and if no person have a majority, then from the two highest numbers on the list, the Senate shall choose the Vice-President; a quorum for the purpose shall consist of two-thirds of the whole number of Senators, and a majority of the whole number shall be necessary to a choice. But no person constitutionally ineligible to the office of President shall be eligible to that of Vice-President of the United States.

The 20th Amendment
(Ratified January 23, 1933)

Section 1. The terms of the President and the Vice President shall end at noon on the 20th day of January, and the terms of Senators and Representatives at noon on the 3d day of January, of the years in which such terms would have ended if this article had not been ratified; and the terms of their successors shall then begin.

Section 2. The Congress shall assemble at least once in every year, and such meeting shall begin at noon on the 3d day of January, unless they shall by law appoint a different day.

Section 3. If, at the time fixed for the beginning of the term of the President, the President elect shall have died, the Vice President elect shall become President. If a President shall not have been chosen before the time fixed for the beginning of his term, or if the President elect shall have failed to qualify, then the Vice President elect shall act as President until a President shall have qualified; and the Congress may by law provide for the case wherein neither a President elect nor a Vice President elect shall have qualified, declaring who shall then act as President, or the manner in which one who is to act shall be selected, and such person shall act accordingly until a President or Vice President shall have qualified.

Section 4. The Congress may by law provide for the case of the death of any of the persons from whom the House of Representatives may choose a President whenever the right of choice shall have devolved upon them, and for the case of the death of any of the persons from whom the Senate may choose a Vice President whenever the right of choice shall have devolved upon them.

The 23rd Amendment
(Ratified March 29, 1961)

Section 1. The District constituting the seat of Government of the United States shall appoint in such manner as the Congress may direct: A number of electors of President and Vice President equal to the whole number of Senators and Representatives in Congress to which the District would be entitled if it were a State, but in no event more than the least populous State; they shall be in addition to those appointed by the States, but they shall be considered, for the purposes of the election of President and Vice President, to be electors appointed by a State; and they shall meet in the District and perform such duties as provided by the twelfth article of amendment.

Appendix B
Statutory Provisions for
Presidential Selection

The following provisions are to be found in Title 3, Chapter 1, of the United States Code (2000 edition), a consolidation and codification of all the general and permanent laws of the United States in force on January 6, 2003. The code consists of 18 volumes (plus an index in seven volumes) and is divided into 50 "titles," organized by subject matter. Thus, Title 3 is titled "The President," and its Chapter 1, "Presidential Elections and Vacancies."

Section 1: Time of appointing electors
The electors of President and Vice President shall be appointed, in each State, on the Tuesday next after the first Monday in November, in every fourth year succeeding every election of a President and Vice President.

Section 2: Failure to make choice on prescribed day
Whenever any State has held an election for the purpose of choosing electors, and has failed to make a choice on the day prescribed by law, the electors may be appointed on a subsequent day in such a manner as the legislature of such State may direct.

Section 3: Number of electors
The number of electors shall be equal to the number of Senators and Representatives to which the several States are by law entitled at the time when the President and Vice President to be chosen come into office; except, that where no apportionment of Representatives has been made after any enumeration, at the time of choosing electors, the number of electors shall be according to the then existing apportionment of Senators and Representatives.

Section 4: Vacancies in electoral college

Each State may, by law, provide for the filling of any vacancies which may occur in its college of electors when such college meets to give its electoral vote.

Section 5: Determination of controversy as to appointment of electors

If any State shall have provided, by laws enacted prior to the day fixed for the appointment of the electors, for its final determination of any controversy or contest concerning the appointment of all or any of the electors of such State, by judicial or other methods or procedures, and such determination shall have been made at least six days before the time fixed for the meeting of the electors, such determination made pursuant to such law so existing on said day, and made at least six days prior to said time of meeting of the electors, shall be conclusive, and shall govern in the counting of the electoral votes as provided in the Constitution, and as hereinafter regulated, so far as the ascertainment of the electors appointed by such State is concerned.

Section 6: Credentials of electors; transmission to Archivist of the United States and to Congress; public inspection

It shall be the duty of the executive of each State, as soon as practicable after the conclusion of the appointment of the electors in such State by the final ascertainment, under and in pursuance of the laws of such State providing for such ascertainment, to communicate by registered mail under the seal of the State to the Archivist of the United States a certificate of such ascertainment of the electors appointed, setting forth the names of such electors and the canvass or other ascertainment under the laws of such State of the number of votes given or cast for each person for whose appointment any and all votes have been given or cast; and it shall also thereupon be the duty of the executive of each State to deliver to the electors of such State, on or before the day on which they are required by section 7 of this title to meet, six duplicate-originals of the same certificate under the seal of the State; and if there shall have been any final determination in a State in the manner provided for by law of a controversy or contest concerning the appointment of all or any of the electors of such State, it shall be the duty of the executive of such State, as soon as practicable after such determination, to communicate under the seal of the State to the Archivist of the United States a certificate of such determination in form and manner as the same shall have been made; and the certificate or certificates so received by the Archivist of the United States shall be preserved by him for one year and shall be a part of the public records of his office and shall be open to public inspection; and the Archivist of the United States at the first meeting of Congress thereafter shall transmit to the two Houses of Congress copies in full of each and every such certificate so received at the National Archives and Records Administration.

Section 7: Meeting and vote of electors

The electors of President and Vice President of each State shall meet and give their votes on the first Monday after the second Wednesday in December next following their appointment at such place in each State as the legislature of such State shall direct.

Section 8: Manner of voting

The electors shall vote for President and Vice President, respectively, in the manner directed by the Constitution.

Section 9: Certificates of votes for President and Vice President

The electors shall make and sign six certificates of all the votes given by them, each of which certificates shall contain two distinct lists, one of the votes for President and the other of the votes for Vice President, and shall annex to each of the certificates one of the lists of the electors which shall have been furnished to them by direction of the executive of the State.

Section 10: Sealing and endorsing certificates

The electors shall seal up the certificates so made by them, and certify upon each that the lists of all the votes of such State given for President, and of all the votes given for Vice President, are contained therein.

Section 11: Disposition of certificates

The electors shall dispose of the certificates so made by them and the lists attached thereto in the following manner:

First. They shall forthwith forward by registered mail one of the same to the President of the Senate at the seat of government.

Second. Two of the same shall be delivered to the secretary of state of the State, one of which shall be held subject to the order of the President of the Senate, the other to be preserved by him for one year and shall be a part of the public records of his office and shall be open to public inspection.

Third. On the day thereafter they shall forward by registered mail two of such certificates and lists to the Archivist of the United States at the seat of government, one of which shall be held subject to the order of the President of the Senate. The other shall be preserved by the Archivist of the United States for one year and shall be a part of the public records of his office and shall be open to public inspection.

Fourth. They shall forthwith cause the other of the certificates and lists to be delivered to the judge of the district in which the electors shall have assembled.

Section 12: Failure of certificates of electors to reach President of the Senate or Archivist of the United States; demand on State for certificate
When no certificate of vote and list mentioned in sections 9 and 11 of this title from any State shall have been received by the President of the Senate or by the Archivist of the United States by the fourth Wednesday in December, after the meeting of the electors shall have been held, the President of the Senate or, if he be absent from the seat of government, the Archivist of the United States shall request, by the most expeditious method available, the secretary of state of the State to send up the certificate and list lodged with him by the electors of such State; and it shall be his duty upon receipt of such request immediately to transmit same by registered mail to the President of the Senate at the seat of government.

Section 13: Same; demand on district judge for certificate
When no certificates of votes from any State shall have been received at the seat of government on the fourth Wednesday in December, after the meeting of the electors shall have been held, the President of the Senate or, if he be absent from the seat of government, the Archivist of the United States shall send a special messenger to the district judge in whose custody

one certificate of votes from that State has been lodged, and such judge shall forthwith transmit that list by the hand of such messenger to the seat of government.

Section 14: Forfeiture for messenger's neglect of duty

Every person who, having been appointed, pursuant to section 13 of this title, to deliver the certificates of the votes of the electors to the President of the Senate, and having accepted such appointment, shall neglect to perform the services required from him, shall forfeit the sum of $1,000.

Section 15: Counting electoral votes in Congress

Congress shall be in session on the sixth day of January succeeding every meeting of the electors. The Senate and House of Representatives shall meet in the Hall of the House of Representatives at the hour of 1 o'clock in the afternoon on that day, and the President of the Senate shall be their presiding officer. Two tellers shall be previously appointed on the part of the Senate and two on the part of the House of Representatives, to whom shall be handed, as they are opened by the President of the Senate, all the certificates and papers purporting to be certificates of the electoral votes, which certificates and papers shall be opened, presented, and acted upon in the alphabetical order of the States, beginning with the letter A; and said tellers, having then read the same in the presence and hearing of the two Houses, shall make a list of the votes as they shall appear from the said certificates; and the votes having been ascertained and counted according to the rules in this subchapter provided, the result of the same shall be delivered to the President of the Senate, who shall thereupon announce the state of the vote, which announcement shall be deemed a sufficient declaration of the persons, if any, elected President and Vice President of the United States, and, together with a list of the votes, be entered on the Journals of the two Houses. Upon such reading of any such certificate or paper, the President of the Senate shall call for objections, if any. Every objection shall be made in writing, and shall state clearly and concisely, and without argument, the ground thereof, and shall be signed by at least one Senator and one Member of the House of Representatives before the same shall be received. When all objections so made to any vote or paper from a State shall have been received and read, the Senate shall thereupon withdraw, and such objections shall be submitted to the Senate for its decision; and the Speaker of the House of Representatives shall, in like manner, submit such objections to the House of Representatives for its decision; and no electoral vote or votes from any State which shall have been regularly given by electors whose appointment has been lawfully certified to according to section 6 of this title from which but one return has been received shall be rejected, but the two Houses concurrently may reject the vote or votes when they agree that such vote or votes have not been so regularly given by electors whose appointment has been so certified. If more than one return or paper purporting to be a return from a State shall have been received by the President of the Senate, those votes, and those only, shall be counted which shall have been regularly given by the electors who are shown by the determination mentioned in section 5 of this title to have been appointed, if the determination in said section provided for shall have been made, or by such successors or substitutes, in case of a vacancy in the board of electors so ascertained, as have been appointed to fill such vacancy in the mode provided by the laws of the State; but in case there shall arise the question which of two or more of such State authorities determining what electors have been appointed, as mentioned in section 5 of this title, is the lawful tribunal of such State, the votes regularly given of those electors, and those only, of such State shall be counted whose title as electors the two Houses, acting separately, shall concurrently decide is supported by the decision of such State so authorized by its law; and in such case of more than one return or paper purporting to be a return from a State, if there shall have been no such determination of the question in the State aforesaid, then those votes, and those only, shall be counted which the two Houses shall concurrently decide were cast by lawful electors appointed in accordance with the laws of the State, unless the two Houses, acting separately, shall concurrently decide such votes not to be the lawful votes of the legally appointed electors of such State. But if the two Houses shall disagree in respect of the counting of such votes, then, and in that case, the votes of the electors whose appointment shall have been certified by the executive of the State, under the seal thereof, shall be counted. When the two Houses have voted, they shall immediately again meet, and the presiding officer shall then announce the decision of the questions submitted. No votes or papers from any other State shall be acted upon until the objections previously made to the votes or papers from any State shall have been finally disposed of.

Section 16: Same; seats for officers and Members of two Houses in joint meeting
At such joint meeting of the two Houses seats shall be provided as follows: For the President of the Senate, the Speaker's chair; for the Speaker, immediately upon his left; the Senators, in the body of the Hall upon the right of the presiding officer; for the Representatives, in the body of the Hall not provided for the Senators; for the tellers, Secretary of the Senate, and Clerk of the House of Representatives, at the Clerk's desk; for the other officers of the two Houses, in front of the Clerk's desk and upon each side of the Speaker's platform. Such joint meeting shall not be dissolved until the count of electoral votes shall be completed and the result declared; and no recess shall be taken unless a question shall have arisen in regard to counting any such votes, or otherwise under this subchapter, in which case it shall be competent for either House, acting separately, in the manner hereinbefore provided, to direct a recess of such House not beyond the next calendar day, Sunday excepted, at the hour of 10 o'clock in the forenoon. But if the counting of the electoral votes and the declaration of the result shall not have been completed before the fifth calendar day next after such first meeting of the two Houses, no further or other recess shall be taken by either House.

Section 17: Same; limit of debate in each House
When the two Houses separate to decide upon an objection that may have been made to the counting of any electoral vote or votes from any State, or other question arising in the matter, each Senator and Representative may speak to such objection or question five minutes, and not more than once; but after such debate shall have lasted two hours it shall be the duty of the presiding officer of each House to put the main question without further debate.

Section 18: Same; parliamentary procedure at joint meeting
While the two Houses shall be in meeting as provided in this chapter, the President of the Senate shall have power to preserve order; and no debate

shall be allowed and no question shall be put by the presiding officer except to either House on a motion to withdraw.

Section 19: Vacancy in offices of both President and Vice President; officers eligible to act

(a) (1) If, by reason of death, resignation, removal from office, inability, or failure to qualify, there is neither a President nor Vice President to discharge the powers and duties of the office of President, then the Speaker of the House of Representatives shall, upon his resignation as Speaker and as Representative in Congress, act as President.

(2) The same rule shall apply in the case of the death, resignation, removal from office, or inability of an individual acting as President under this subsection.

(b) If, at the time when under subsection (a) of this section a Speaker is to begin the discharge of the powers and duties of the office of President, there is no Speaker, or the Speaker fails to qualify as Acting President, then the President pro tempore of the Senate shall, upon his resignation as President pro tempore and as Senator, act as President.

(c) An individual acting as President under subsection (a) or subsection (b) of this section shall continue to act until the expiration of the then current Presidential term, except that

(1) if his discharge of the powers and duties of the office is founded in whole or in part on the failure of both the President-elect and the Vice-President-elect to qualify, then he shall act only until a President or Vice President qualifies; and

(2) if his discharge of the powers and duties of the office is founded in whole or in part on the inability of the President or Vice President, then he shall act only until the removal of the disability of one of such individuals.

(d) (1) If, by reason of death, resignation, removal from office, inability, or failure to qualify, there is no President pro tempore to act as President under subsection (b) of this section, then the officer of the United States who is highest on the following list, and who is not under disability to discharge the powers and duties of the office of President shall act as President: Secretary of State, Secretary of the Treasury, Secretary of Defense, Attorney General, Secretary of the Interior, Secretary of Agriculture, Secretary of Commerce, Secretary of Labor, Secretary of Health and Human Services, Secretary of Housing and Urban Development, Secretary of Transportation, Secretary of Energy, Secretary of Education, Secretary of Veterans Affairs, Secretary of Homeland Security.

(2) An individual acting as President under this subsection shall continue so to do until the expiration of the then current Presidential term, but not after a qualified and prior entitled individual is able to act, except that the removal of the disability of an individual higher on the list contained in paragraph (1) of this subsection or the ability to qualify on the part of an individual higher on such list shall not terminate his service.

(3) The taking of the oath of office by an individual specified in the list in paragraph (1) of this subsection shall be held to constitute his resignation from the office by virtue of the holding of which he qualifies to act as President.

(e) Subsections (a), (b), and (d) of this section shall apply only to such officers as are eligible to the office of President under the Constitution. Subsection (d) of this section shall apply only to officers appointed, by and with the advice and consent of the Senate, prior to the time of the death, resignation, removal from office, inability, or failure to qualify, of the President pro tempore, and only to officers not under impeachment by the House of Representatives at the time the powers and duties of the office of President devolve upon them.

(f) During the period that any individual acts as President under this section, his compensation shall be at the rate then provided by law in the case of the President.

Section 20: Resignation or refusal of office

The only evidence of a refusal to accept, or of a resignation of the office of President or Vice President, shall be an instrument in writing, declaring the same, and subscribed by the person refusing to accept or resigning, as the case may be, and delivered into the office of the Secretary of State.

Appendix C

Nomination and Binding of
Presidential Electors

State	Candidates for Elector Are Nominated by	Are Electors' Names on Ballot?	Are Electors Bound?	Penalty
Alabama	CN	N	Y	No Penalty
Alaska	PO	N	Y	No Penalty
Arizona	*	Y	Y	Replace
Arkansas	CN	N	N	—
California	*	N	Y	Replace
Colorado	CN	N	Y	Replace
Connecticut	PO	N	Y	No Penalty
Delaware	CN	N	Y	No Penalty
District of Columbia	CO	N	Y	No Penalty
Florida	CO	N	Y	No Penalty
Georgia	CN	N	N	—
Hawaii	CN	N	Y	No Penalty
Idaho	CN	Y	N	—
Illinois	PO	N	N	—
Indiana	CN	N	Y	Replace
Iowa	PO	N	N	—
Kansas	CO	N	N	—
Kentucky	PO	N	N	—
Louisiana	PO	Y	N	—
Maine	CN	N	Y	Replace
Maryland	PO	N	Y	No Penalty
Massachusetts	CO	N	Y	No Penalty
Michigan	CN	N	Y	Replace
Minnesota	CN	N	Y	Replace
Mississippi	CN	N	Y	No Penalty

(Continued on next page)

(Continued from previous page)

State	Candidates for Elector Are Nominated by	Are Electors' Names on Ballot?	Are Electors Bound?	Penalty
Missouri	CO	N	N	—
Montana	PO	N	Y	Replace
Nebraska	CN	N	Y	Replace
Nevada	CN	N	Y	Replace
New Hampshire	CN	N	N	—
New Jersey	CO	N	N	—
New Mexico	CN	N	Y	Fine
New York	CO	N	N	—
North Carolina	CN	N	Y	Fine, Replace
North Dakota	CN	Y	N	—
Ohio	CN	N	Y	No Penalty
Oklahoma	CN	Y	Y	Fine, Replace
Oregon	PO	N	Y	No Penalty
Pennsylvania	*	N	N	—
Rhode Island	CN	N	N	—
South Carolina	CO	N	Y	Fine
South Dakota	CN	Y	N	—
Tennessee	PO	N	Y	No Penalty
Texas	PO	N	N	—
Utah	PO	N	Y	Replace
Vermont	CN	N	Y	No Penalty
Virginia	CN	N	Y	No Penalty
Washington	CN	N	Y	Replace
West Virginia	CN	N	N	—
Wisconsin	*	N	Y	No Penalty
Wyoming	CN	N	Y	No Penalty

Note: PO: party option; CN: party convention; CO: party committee; N: No; Y: Yes; Fine: An elector is fined for casting a faithless vote; Replace: an elector is removed and replaced for casting a faithless vote; No Penalty: electors are bound, but there is no penalty for casting a faithless vote.

Source: Author's compilation from state election codes. See also FairVote, "Faithless Elector State Laws," July 7, 2020, https://www.fairvote.org/faithless_elector_state_laws.

Appendix D

1825 Precedents

The following rules, reprinted from Hinds' Precedents of the House of Representatives, *were adopted by the House in 1825 for use in deciding the choice of a president, when, as then, choice devolved upon the House.*

Hinds' Precedents Volume 3, Chapter 62, § 1984

1. In the event of its appearing, on opening all the certificates, and counting the votes given by the electors of the several States for President, that no person has a majority of the votes of the whole number of electors appointed, the same shall be entered on the Journals of this House.

2. The roll of the House shall then be called by States; and, on its appearing that a Member or Members from two-thirds of the States are present, the House shall immediately proceed, by ballot, to choose a President from the persons having the highest numbers, not exceeding three, on the list of those voted for as President; and, in case neither of those persons shall receive the votes of a majority of all the States on the first ballot, the House shall continue to ballot for a President, without interruption by other business, until a President be chosen.

3. The doors of the Hall shall be closed during the balloting, except against the Members of the Senate, stenographers, and the officers of the House.

4. From the commencement of the balloting until an election is made no proposition to adjourn shall be received, unless on

the motion of one State, seconded by another State, and the question shall be decided by States. The same rule shall be observed in regard to any motion to change the usual hour for the meeting of the House.

5. In balloting the following mode shall be observed, to wit:

The Representatives of each State shall be arranged and seated together, beginning with the seats at the right hand of the Speaker's chair, with the Members from the State of Maine; thence, proceeding with the Members from the States, in the order the States are usually named for receiving petitions, around the Hall of the House, until all are seated.

A ballot box shall be provided for each State.

The Representatives of each State shall, in the first instance, ballot among themselves, in order to ascertain the vote of their State; and they may, if necessary, appoint tellers of their ballots.

After the vote of each State is ascertained, duplicates thereof shall be made out; and in case any one of the persons from whom the choice is to be made shall receive a majority of the votes given, on any one balloting by the Representatives of a State, the name of that person shall be written on each of the duplicates; and in case the votes so given shall be divided so that neither of said persons shall have a majority of the whole number of votes given by such State, on any one balloting, then the word "divided" shall be written on each duplicate.

After the delegation from each State shall have ascertained the vote of their State, the Clerk shall name the States in the order they are usually named for receiving petitions; and as the name of each is called the Sergeant-at-Arms shall present to the delegation of each two ballot boxes, in each of which shall be deposited, by some Representative of the State, one of the duplicates made as aforesaid of the vote of said State, in the presence and subject to the examination of all the Members from said State then present; and where there is more than one Representative from a State, the duplicates shall not both be deposited by the same person.

When the votes of the States are thus all taken in, the Sergeant-at-Arms shall carry one of said ballot boxes to one table and the other to a separate and distinct table.

One person from each State represented in the balloting shall be appointed by the Representatives to tell off said ballots; but, in case the Representatives fail to appoint a teller, the Speaker shall appoint.

The said tellers shall divide themselves into two sets, as nearly equal in number as can be, and one of the said sets of tellers shall proceed to count the votes in one of said boxes, and the other set the votes in the other box.

When the votes are counted by the different sets of tellers, the result shall be reported to the House; and if the reports agree, the same shall be accepted as the true votes of the States; but if the reports disagree, the States shall proceed, in the same manner as before, to a new ballot.

6. All questions arising after the balloting commences, requiring the decision of the House, which shall be decided by the House, voting per capita, to be incidental to the power of choosing a President, shall be decided by States without debate; and in case of an equal division of the votes of States, the question shall be lost.

7. When either of the persons from whom the choice is to be made shall have received a majority of all the States, the Speaker shall declare the same, and that that person is elected President of the United States.

8. The result shall be immediately communicated to the Senate by message, and a committee of three persons shall be appointed to inform the President of the United States and the President-elect of said election.

Appendix E

Party Rules

Charter and Bylaws of the Democratic Party, Article III, Section 1
The Democratic National Committee shall have general responsibility for the affairs of the Democratic Party between National Conventions, subject to the provisions of this Charter and to the resolutions or other actions of the National Convention. This responsibility shall include . . . filling vacancies in the nominations for the office of President and Vice President.

Rule 9 of the Republican Party, Filling Vacancies in Nominations
(a) The Republican National Committee is hereby authorized and empowered to fill any and all vacancies which may occur by reason of death, declination, or otherwise of the Republican candidate for President of the United States or the Republican candidate for Vice President of the United States, as nominated by the national convention, or the Republican National Committee may reconvene the national convention for the purpose of filling any such vacancies.

(b) In voting under this rule, the Republican National Committee members representing any state shall be entitled to cast the same number of votes as said state was entitled to cast at the national convention.

(c) In the event that the members of the Republican National Committee from any state shall not be in agreement in the casting of votes hereunder, the votes of such state shall be divided equally, including fractional votes, among the members of the Republican National Committee present or voting by proxy.

(d) No candidate shall be chosen to fill any such vacancy except upon receiving a majority of the votes entitled to be cast in the election.

Appendix F

Electoral Votes for the States for 2020

State	Number of Electoral Votes	State	Number of Electoral Votes
Alabama	9	Montana	3
Alaska	3	Nebraska	5
Arizona	11	Nevada	6
Arkansas	6	New Hampshire	4
California	55	New Jersey	14
Colorado	9	New Mexico	5
Connecticut	7	New York	29
Delaware	3	North Carolina	15
District of Columbia	3	North Dakota	3
Florida	29	Ohio	18
Georgia	16	Oklahoma	7
Hawaii	4	Oregon	7
Idaho	4	Pennsylvania	20
Illinois	20	Rhode Island	4
Indiana	11	South Carolina	9
Iowa	6	South Dakota	3
Kansas	6	Tennessee	11
Kentucky	8	Texas	38
Louisiana	8	Utah	6
Maine	4	Vermont	3
Maryland	10	Virginia	13
Massachusetts	11	Washington	12
Michigan	16	West Virginia	5
Minnesota	10	Wisconsin	10
Mississippi	6	Wyoming	3
Missouri	10		
		Total	**538**

Source: US National Archives and Records Administration.

Appendix G

Faithless Electors

Year	Name	State	Expected Vote	Actual Vote
1796	Samuel Miles	Pennsylvania	John Adams (F)	Thomas Jefferson (DR)
1808	6 anonymous	New York	James Madison (DR)	George Clinton (DR)
1820	William Plummer Sr	New Hampshire	James Monroe (DR)	John Quincy Adams(DR)
1832	2 anonymous	Maryland	Henry Clay (NR)	Abstention
1892	1 anonymous	Oregon	Benjamin Harrison (R)	James B. Weaver (P)
1948	Preston Parks	Tennessee	Harry Truman (D)	Strom Thurmond (States' Rights)
1956	W. F. Turner	Alabama	Adlai Stevenson (D)	Walter Burgwyn Jones (D)
1960	Henry D. Irwin	Oklahoma	Richard Nixon (R)	Harry Byrd (D)
1968	Lloyd W. Bailey	North Carolina	Richard Nixon (R)	George Wallace (American Independent)
1972	Roger L. MacBride	Virginia	Richard Nixon (R)	John Hospers (Libertarian)
1976	Mike Padden	Washington	Gerald Ford (R)	Ronald Reagan (R)
1988	Margaret Leach	West Virginia	Michael Dukakis (D)	Lloyd Bentsen (D)

(Continued on next page)

(Continued from previous page)

Year	Name	State	Expected Vote	Actual Vote
2000	Barbara Lett-Simmons	District of Columbia	Al Gore (D)	Abstention
2004	1 anonymous	Minnesota	John Kerry (D)	John Edwards (D)
2016	Bret Chiafolo	Washington	Hillary Clinton (D)	Colin Powell (R)
2016	Levi Guerra	Washington	Hillary Clinton (D)	Colin Powell (R)
2016	Esther John	Washington	Hillary Clinton (D)	Colin Powell (R)
2016	Robert Satiacum	Washington	Hillary Clinton (D)	Faith Spotted Eagle
2016	David Mulinix	Hawaii	Hillary Clinton (D)	Bernie Sanders (D)
2016	Christopher Suprun	Texas	Donald Trump (R)	John Kasich (R)
2016	Bill Greene	Texas	Donald Trump (R)	Ron Paul (Libertarian)

Source: Congressional Research Service; and US National Archives and Records Administration.

Appendix H

Electoral College and Popular Vote Outcomes of All Elections

Year	Candidates	Party	Electoral Vote	Popular Vote
2016	Donald Trump	Republican	304	62,985,134
	Hillary Clinton	Democrat	227	65,853,652
2012	Barack Obama	Democrat	332	65,918,507
	Mitt Romney	Republican	206	60,934,407
2008	Barack Obama	Democrat	365	69,499,428
	John McCain	Republican	173	59,950,323
2004	George W. Bush	Republican	286	62,039,572
	John Kerry	Democrat	251	59,027,117
2000	George W. Bush	Republican	271	50,460,110
	Albert Gore	Democrat	266	51,003,926
1996	Bill Clinton	Democrat	379	47,400,125
	Robert Dole	Republican	159	37,198,755
1992	Bill Clinton	Democrat	370	44,909,806
	George H. W. Bush	Republican	168	44,104,550
1988	George H. W. Bush	Republican	426	48,886,597
	Michael Dukakis	Democrat	111	41,809,476

(Continued on next page)

(Continued from previous page)

Year	Candidates	Party	Electoral Vote	Popular Vote
1984	Ronald Reagan	Republican	525	54,455,472
	Walter Mondale	Democrat	13	37,577,352
1980	Ronald Reagan	Republican	489	43,903,230
	Jimmy Carter	Democrat	49	35,480,115
1976	Jimmy Carter	Democrat	297	40,831,881
	Gerald Ford	Republican	240	39,148,634
1972	Richard Nixon	Republican	520	47,163,710
	George McGovern	Democrat	17	29,173,222
1968	Richard Nixon	Republican	301	31,783,783
	Hubert Humphrey	Democrat	191	31,271,839
	George Wallace	American Independent	46	9,901,118
1964	Lyndon Johnson	Democrat	486	43,127,041
	Barry Goldwater	Republican	52	27,175,754
1960	John F. Kennedy	Democrat	303	34,221,349
	Richard Nixon	Republican	219	34,108,546
	Unpledged Electors	Democrat	15	286,359
1956	Dwight Eisenhower	Republican	457	34,221,349
	Adlai Stevenson	Democrat	73	26,028,028
1952	Dwight Eisenhower	Republican	442	33,778,963
	Adlai Stevenson	Democrat	89	27,314,992
1948	Harry Truman	Democrat	303	24,075,529
	Thomas Dewey	Republican	189	21,991,292
	J. Strom Thurmond	States' Rights	39	1,175,930
1944	Franklin D. Roosevelt	Democrat	432	25,612,916
	Thomas Dewey	Republican	99	22,017,929

(Continued on next page)

(Continued from previous page)

Year	Candidates	Party	Electoral Vote	Popular Vote
1940	Franklin D. Roosevelt	Democrat	449	27,313,945
	Wendell Willkie	Republican	82	22,347,744
1936	Franklin D. Roosevelt	Democrat	523	27,752,949
	Alfred Landon	Republican	8	16,683,293
1932	Franklin D. Roosevelt	Democrat	472	22,821,857
	Herbert Hoover	Republican	59	15,761,586
1928	Herbert Hoover	Republican	444	21,427,123
	Alfred E. Smith	Democrat	87	15,015,464
1924	Calvin Coolidge	Republican	382	15,723,789
	John W. Davis	Democrat	136	8,386,242
	Robert LaFollette	Progressive	13	4,831,706
1920	Warren Harding	Republican	404	16,147,885
	James Cox	Democrat	127	9,141,535
1916	Woodrow Wilson	Democrat	277	9,126,868
	Charles Hughes	Republican	254	8,548,728
1912	Woodrow Wilson	Democrat	435	6,296,184
	Teddy Roosevelt	Progressive	88	4,122,721
	William Howard Taft	Republican	8	3,486,242
1908	William Howard Taft	Republican	321	7,678,395
	William J. Bryan	Democrat	162	6,408,948
1904	Teddy Roosevelt	Republican	336	7,630,457
	Alton Parker	Democrat	140	5,083,880
1900	William McKinley	Republican	292	7,228,864
	William J. Bryan	Democratic-Populist	155	6,370,932
1896	William McKinley	Republican	271	7,112,138
	William J. Bryan	Democratic-Populist	176	6,508,172

(Continued on next page)

(Continued from previous page)

Year	Candidates	Party	Electoral Vote	Popular Vote
1892	Grover Cleveland	Democrat	277	5,553,898
	Benjamin Harrison	Republican	145	5,190,819
	James Weaver	Populist	22	1,026,595
1888	Benjamin Harrison	Republican	233	5,443,892
	Grover Cleveland	Democrat	168	5,534,488
1884	Grover Cleveland	Democrat	219	4,874,621
	James Blaine	Republican	182	4,848,936
1880	James Garfield	Republican	214	4,446,158
	Winfield Hancock	Democrat	155	4,444,260
1876	Rutherford Hayes	Republican	185	4,034,311
	Samuel Tilden	Democrat	184	4,288,546
1872	Ulysses Grant	Republican	286	3,598,235
	Horace Greeley	Democratic-Liberal Republican	66*	2,834,761
1868	Ulysses Grant	Republican	214	8,013,650
	Horatio Seymour	Democrat	80	2,708,774
1864	Abraham Lincoln	Republican	212	2,218,388
	George McClellan	Democrat	21	1,812,807
	Nonvoting Elector		1	
1860	Abraham Lincoln	Republican	180	1,856,908
	John Breckinridge	S. Democrat	72	848,019
	John Bell	Constitution Union	39	590,901
	Stephen Douglas	Democrat	12	1,380,202
1856	James Buchanan	Democrat	174	1,836,072
	John C. Fremont	Republican	114	1,342,345
	Millard Fillmore	American	8	873,053
1852	Franklin Pierce	Democrat	254	1,607,510
	Winfield Scott	Whig	42	1,386,942
1848	Zachary Taylor	Whig	163	1,361,393
	Lewis Cass	Democrat	127	1,223,460

(Continued on next page)

(Continued from previous page)

Year	Candidates	Party	Electoral Vote	Popular Vote
1844	James Polk	Democrat	170	1,339,494
	Henry Clay	Whig	105	1,300,004
1840	William Henry Harrison	Whig	234	1,275,390
	Martin Van Buren	Democrat	60	1,128,884
1836	Martin Van Buren	Democrat	170	764,176
	William Henry Harrison	Whig	73	550,816
	Hugh White	Whig	26	146,107
	Daniel Webster	Whig	14	41,201
	Willie Mangum	Whig	11	0
1832	Andrew Jackson	Democrat	219	701,780
	Henry Clay	National-Republican	49	484,205
	John Floyd	Ind. Democrat	11	0
	William Wirt	Anti-Masonic	7	100,715
1828	Andrew Jackson	Democrat	178	642,553
	John Quincy Adams	National-Republican	83	500,897
1824	John Quincy Adams	Coalition	84	113,122
	Andrew Jackson	Democratic-Republican	99	151,271
	William Crawford	Democratic-Republican	41	40,856
	Henry Clay	Democratic-Republican	37	47,531
1820	James Monroe	Democratic-Republican	231	No Record
	John Quincy Adams	National-Republican	1	
	Nonvoting Electors		3	
1816	James Monroe	Democratic-Republican	183	No Record
	Rufus King	Federalist	34	
	Nonvoting Electors		4	
1812	James Madison	Democratic-Republican	128	No Record
	DeWitt Clinton	Federalist	89	
	Nonvoting Elector		1	

(Continued on next page)

(Continued from previous page)

Year	Candidates	Party	Electoral Vote	Popular Vote
1808	James Madison	Democratic-Republican	122	No Record
	Charles Pinckney	Federalist	47	
	George Clinton	Democratic-Republican	6	
	Nonvoting Elector		1	
1804	Thomas Jefferson	Democratic-Republican	162	No Record
	Charles Pinckney	Federalist	14	
1800	Thomas Jefferson	Democratic-Republican	73	No Record
	Aaron Burr	Democratic-Republican	73	
	John Adams	Federalist	65	
	Charles Pinckney	Federalist	64	
	John Jay	Federalist	1	
1796	John Adams	Federalist	71	No Record
	Thomas Jefferson	Democratic-Republican	68	
	Thomas Pinckney	Federalist	59	
	Aaron Burr	Democratic-Republican	30	
	Samuel Adams	Federalist	15	
	Oliver Ellsworth	Federalist	11	
	George Clinton	Democratic-Republican	7	
	Others		15	
1792	George Washington	Federalist	132	No Record
	John Adams	Federalist	7	
	George Clinton	Democratic-Republican	50	
	Thomas Jefferson	Democratic-Republican	4	
	Aaron Burr	Democratic-Republican	1	
	Electors Not Cast		6	
1789	George Washington		69	No Record
	John Adams		34	
	John Jay		9	
	Robert Harrison		6	
	John Rutledge		6	
	Others		14	
	Electors Not Cast		24	

Note: This chart does not include third-party candidates who did not receive any electoral votes. *Horace Greeley died before the electors cast their votes. Their votes were split among several Democratic candidates. In addition to the 266 electors for Grant, 14 electors for Grant from Louisiana and Arkansas were rejected due to election irregularities.

Source: Dave Leip, *Atlas of U.S. Presidential Elections*, www.uselectionatlas.org.